APA Essentials

7th Edition: Style, Formatting, and Grammar

APA Essentials

7th Edition: Style, Formatting, and Grammar

Dona J. Young

cognella®

SAN DIEGO

Bassim Hamadeh, CEO and Publisher
Amy Smith, Senior Project Editor
Celeste Paed, Associate Production Editor
Jess Estrella, Senior Graphic Designer
Kylie Bartolome, Licensing Coordinator
Stephanie Adams, Senior Marketing Program Manager
Natalie Piccotti, Director of Marketing
Kassie Graves, Senior Vice President, Editorial
Jamie Giganti, Director of Academic Publishing

3970 Sorrento Valley Blvd., Ste. 500, San Diego, CA 92121

To the curious mind in search of truth and clarity.

BRIEF CONTENTS

DETAILED CONTENTS

INTRODUCTION

Though the American Psychological Association (APA) citation system and writing style is one of the most widely used citation systems in the world, it is generally not used in English classes. Instead, writers use APA in the social and health sciences for academic papers and articles submitted for publication. Therefore, when you write your first paper for a class outside of the humanities, you may find yourself at a loss citing and formatting your work.

APA has a unique structure, which is quite different from Modern Library Association (MLA) style, so you might experience some growing pains until you learn the basics. However, using APA correctly offers many benefits, including the following:

- Quoting and citing resources correctly adds richness and credibility to your work.
- Formatting your work correctly lets readers know at first glance you have made the effort to get it right, which conveys respect.
- Citing your research not only validates your findings but also provides others with information to find your source, enabling them to read the entire resource.

APA style also provides professionals with a shared language or code, much like commonly known abbreviations or texting vernacular do. This consistency enables professionals to review literature effectively.

This book walks you through the basics and provides tips on APA style, formatting, and citation as well as grammar. However, covering all elements of APA style is beyond the scope and mission of this book; this book is designed to get you started on a path to using APA that brings you success. For advice on advanced work and complicated references, refer to the *Publication Manual of the American Psychological Association,* 7th edition (2020). Though the author and editors have done their best to ensure accuracy, APA style is complicated, and some points may differ due to interpretation.

PART I

Style, Formatting, and Grammar

1

APA CITATION STYLE

A Few Basics

American Psychological Association (APA) style is unique, and an informed reader can see formatting and stylistic errors at a glance; when you get APA style right, you're likely to gain instant credibility with your reader. However, when you start using APA style, it can seem confusing and even overwhelming. As a starting point, this chapter provides a brief overview of key elements of APA style, which will be more fully developed in later chapters.

Even if you have used APA style in the past, it isn't safe to assume you've been using it correctly. For example, most professors focus on the content of your work and do not give detailed feedback on writing errors. In addition, in the 7th edition of its publication manual, APA made distinct changes to citation and formatting as well as grammar and word usage. For best results, take a fresh look at the requirements presented in the *Publication Manual of the American Psychological Association*, 7th edition (American Psychological Association [APA], 2020b). Its index is helpful for finding precise and detailed information about all the topics it discusses.

A multitude of disciplines require APA style, such as the social sciences and health care; in fact, APA may be the most widely used citation system in the world (Schultz, 2019). Thus, by getting APA style correct now, you are making an excellent investment in your academic writing, readying your skills to present articles for professional publication.

When you complete this chapter, you will

- understand the basics of APA citation style,
- know the difference between narrative and parenthetical citations,
- know which types of information to credit,
- be able to create a working reference list (or working bibliography),
- be able to identify the difference between summarizing and paraphrasing, and
- appreciate the costs of plagiarism.

APA Citation Style

APA style may seem challenging at first, especially if you are accustomed to Modern Library Association (MLA) style, which is used in the humanities, such as English classes. APA even has unique grammar rules that differ from some other citation systems, such as the adoption of the singular "they" in their most recent edition. To help you get acquainted, let's start by covering a few points that make APA style unique.

A Few Basics

To get oriented to APA style and its unique terms and features, the following are a few key points to consider:

- APA citation style is an *in-text citation* system, which means author–date references are placed in the body of the text.
- APA requires that writers refer to authors by last name only (e.g., "Barnard found that …"). In references, use initials in place of first names (for example, "N. Barnard"). By using only last names and initials, gender bias is removed.
- APA uses both narrative citations and parenthetical citations:
  - A *narrative citation* uses an author's name in the text of the writing (not in parentheses) and frequently also uses the year of publication in the text:
    - Fitch (2018) concluded that more research was needed.

- In 2017, Adams concluded more information was needed to determine causality.
- A *parenthetical citation* includes citation information in parentheses and most often occurs at the end of a sentence (but should always appear after the source being discussed and can, therefore, occur elsewhere when multiple topics are discussed in the same sentence):
  - More research was needed (Fitch, 2018), and the decision was made to fund the proposal.
  - More research was needed to determine causality (Adams, 2017).
- For references, use a *reference page* (not a works cited page or bibliography). Though you may refer to a variety of sources as you do your research, when using APA style, list only those references you cite in your work.
- APA uses gender-neutral pronouns, such as the singular "they." Therefore, do not use "he" or "she" or their related forms when referring to a person of unknown gender identity or as generic pronouns.
- APA also uses gender-neutral language for gender identity and sexual orientation as well as unbiased language for race, ethnicity, and disability.
- APA formatting uses double spacing throughout the entire document, including the title page, abstract, body, and reference page.
- While APA 6th edition recommended spacing two times after a period, APA 7th edition recommends spacing one time after a period.
- APA gives the option of six styles of font from which to choose. Once you select a font, use only that font for all parts of your paper, including the header (if you include one) and the reference page.
  - Do not use a larger font for your title page or charts and graphs.
  - Do not use color to make parts of your paper stand out, such as by putting headings in color.

Parts of an APA Paper

In general, an APA paper contains four major sections:

- title page
- abstract
- main body
- reference page

For an experimental report, the main body consists of the following parts:

- method
- results
- discussion

For research papers, the main body of the paper includes the following:

- review of literature
- research methods
- findings and analysis
- discussion
- limitations
- future scope

Narrative and Parenthetical Citations

APA style requires in-text citations, using narrative (in the body of the sentence) or parenthetical citations (generally at the end of the sentence).

TABLE 1.1 **APA In-Text Citations**

Author	Narrative Citation	Parenthetical Citation
One author	According to Tadeuz (2018), the study …	(Tadeuz, 2018)
	A comparison of a study by Perez (2019) and a study by Thomas (2016) revealed that …	(Perez, 2019; Thomas, 2016)

(continued)

TABLE 1.1 **APA In-Text Citations** (*Continued*)

Author	Narrative Citation	Parenthetical Citation
Two authors	Edgar and Johnston (2018) found that …	(Edgar & Johnston, 2018)
	T. Pietro and R. D. Pietro (2020) studied …	(T. Pietro & R. D. Pietro, 2020)
Three or more authors	In a study by Greger et al. (2018), they found similar …	(Greger et al., 2018)
Group author with abbreviation (first citation)	In 2020, the American Psychological Association (APA) …	(American Psychological Association [APA], 2020)
Group author with abbreviation (subsequent citations)	In 2020, APA …	(APA, 2020)
Group author with no abbreviation	Indiana University (2020)	(Indiana University, 2020)
No author	Title (date)	("Title," date)
No author and title	Author (n.d.)	(Author, n.d.)

To adapt to in-text citation, you must also adapt your writing style. One way to coach yourself is using sentence prompts to structure your ideas. The University of Manchester's "Academic Phrasebank" provides a multitude of examples that can help ease you into building your academic vocabulary, such as the following ("Academic Phrasebank," n.d.):

Reinhart (2018)	found	distinct	differences between X and Y.
	observed	significant	
		considerable	
		major	
		only slight	

APA style requires that sources cited in the text are listed on a reference page at the end of the work. These references provide readers with complete information to access your original source. If you would like to comment on or provide supplementary information to your text, APA allows you to provide such information in footnotes.

If you find yourself stuck on a challenging reference, remember to refer to the *Publication Manual of the American Psychological Association*, 7th edition (APA, 2020b) or one of the several online citation generators. If you use a citation generator, do not simply copy and paste it to your reference page; check that the citation includes all the appropriate information, remove the website's formatting, and set the citation in hanging indentation format with the correct font style and size.

Citation Examples

The following are a few examples of different citation forms:

- For narrative citations, follow authors' names with the publication year in parentheses:
    - Klaper and Esselstyn (2016) found that modifying diet resulted in lower blood pressure.
- For parenthetical citations, enclose authors' names and year of publication in parentheses at the end of the sentence:
    - Modifying diet resulted in lower blood pressure (Klaper & Esselstyn, 2016).
- When the authors' names and publication year are part of the narrative, that is sufficient. For subsequent narrative citation within the same paragraph, the date is not necessary; however, use the date for all parenthetical citations:
    - In 2016, Klaper and Esselstyn's study showed lower blood pressure for the modified diet.
- When a work has two authors, cite both names each time they are referenced:
    - McDougall and Greger (2017) conducted nutrition-based studies.
- When a work has three or more authors, use only the surname of the first author followed by "et al." (but do not use "et al." on the reference page):
    - Melchiori et al. (2018) demonstrated that additional research was warranted.

- For short quotations, place the reference inside of the period, and include the page number:
  - "Additional studies are needed to fill the gap" (Melchiori, 2018, p. 33).
- For quotations longer than 40 words, indent the left margin 0.5 inches, and do not use quotation marks. Because the quotation is set off from the rest of the text, place the citation on the outside of the period.

What to Credit

Not all information needs to be documented. For example, you do not need to cite information that is considered common knowledge or facts that are available from a wide variety of sources. According to *The New St. Martin's Handbook*, the following information should be documented:

- direct quotations and paraphrases
- information that is not widely known or claims that are not agreed upon
- judgments, opinions, and claims of others
- statistics, charts, tables, and graphs from any source
- help provided by friends, instructors, or others (Lundsford & Connors, 2001)

In academic settings, you must also cite your own work from another course or article. Also, when turning in group projects, identify who provided information on each presentation slide. In other words, be careful not to claim the writing of another group participant as your work.

The two most common types of references are direct quotations and paraphrases. A *direct quotation* refers to using someone else's exact words, and it requires the words to be set off. For short quotes, use quotation marks; for quotes of 40 or more words, set off the quotation by indenting the left margin 0.5 inches. Use an in-text reference along with a citation on the reference page. *Paraphrasing* refers to putting someone else's ideas in your own words so that you can explain how their ideas support or oppose your topic. When you paraphrase and cite your source, you add credibility to your work. Making a few changes to word order, leaving out a word or two, or substituting similar words needs citation, or it is considered *plagiarism*.

While academic standards require you to provide evidence to support a position, use quotations selectively. Just as a quote in exactly the right place can enhance your work, too many quotes or unnecessary ones can distract your readers and may imply you do not fully understand the topic. Aim for flow, and be selective.

Summarizing and Paraphrasing

Even when you write about someone's ideas in your own words, you still need to cite the original source. Summarizing and paraphrasing can easily be mistaken for one another. The following are the differences between the two:

- When you paraphrase, you are "translating" an original piece of writing but not copying any parts word for word. To paraphrase, read material, assimilate it, write about concepts in your own words, and credit the original author.
- When you *summarize*, you are putting the most important elements of the original writing into your own words.

If you are not confident about your writing skills, you may be tempted to integrate many quotes into your writing. Instead, as a writer, you need to develop your voice, which enables you to interpret information in your own words. You can take the following steps to begin developing your voice:

1. To paraphrase or summarize, first read the original source.
2. Read and analyze as many times as needed. Scholarly sources can be time-consuming to fully comprehend.
3. Write a few notes—in your own words—about what the author is saying.
4. Put away the original source, and write your summary.
5. If you have trouble paraphrasing, break it down by reading a section, cover it, and then write the explanation.

6. You can also explain to someone what you think the writer means, and then write it in your own words.
7. Always remember, it's alright to ask for help.

Once again, use quotations selectively; write until you have clarity. Rather than using your ideas to support quotations, use quotations to support your thesis. Do you see the difference? After you write your summary, look back at the original source. Did you capture the original concepts and integrate your own interpretation into your writing?

READING, REFLECTING, WRITING

The more you read and reflect and write from your own voice, the stronger your skills become. That's true even when writing feels like a struggle, which can be a good sign because it means that you are making progress. When you feel overwhelmed, put your work aside for a short time, and then go back to it. Here are a few more tips:

- Think of reading as a form of meditation. Jot down your ideas and insights as you read.

- Don't copy anything directly from the reading, unless you plan to use it as a direct quotation. Use quotations sparingly, and make sure to write your full reference.

- Close your book and your notes before you start composing.

Working Bibliography

Citing research can be challenging because it involves details. Therefore, as you collect and use what others have discovered, compile a working list of references. As you collect your research, use a separate file on your computer, note cards, or a small notebook.

To make citing your sources manageable, use reference management software that helps organize resources. Tools such as RefWorks, EndNote, and Zotero will insert citations into your document as you write, as will Microsoft Word. Endnote also allows you to save electronic documents, your comment notes, and keywords so that you can search your downloaded documents. Zotero is free and open source, and it is recommended for advanced undergraduate students, graduate students, and faculty.

If you use reference management software, be sure to set it to APA 7th edition, if it is available. If you use APA 6th edition, review the changes against the 7th edition, and correct your citations manually. Also learn how to insert page and paragraph numbers into the citation when you cite quotes.

The following is the kind of information you need to collect:

- **books and e-books**
  - ○ author, title, and page number (italicize book titles); include up to 20 authors in a reference list entry
  - ○ publisher and year of publication (APA no longer requires location of publisher)
  - ○ digital object identifier DOI and URL, if available, which is a string of numbers, letters, and symbols used to identify an article or document and link it on the web

American Psychological Association. (2020). *Publication manual of the American Psychological Association* (7th ed.). https://doi.org/10.1037/0000165-000

- **periodicals**
  - ○ author and title of article (do not italicize the titles of journal articles)
  - ○ journal title, date of publication, volume, and issue number (italicize the titles of journals along with the volume number)
  - ○ DOI and URL, if available

Fauteux, N. (2021). Covid-19: Impact on nurses and nursing. *American Journal of Nursing, 121*(5), 19–21. https://doi.org/10.1097/01.naj.0000751076.87046.19

- **webpages and online data**
  - ○ author (if known) and title
  - ○ DOI and URL, if available

- ○ retrieval date (if no DOI is available)
- ○ URL network address, which includes path and file names enclosed in angle brackets
- ○ date website was established (if available; usually located at bottom of the home page)
- ○ date the source was published in print (if previously published)
- ○ paragraph number (if you quote from a website)
- ○ a printed hard copy or downloaded copy of the material you are referencing because electronic sources are ever changing

National Association for Healthcare Quality. (2022). *Code of ethics for healthcare quality professionals*. Retrieved April 30, 2022, from https://nahq.org/about-nahq/code-of-ethics/

Reference List

Use the following formatting for your reference list:

- Align the first line of each entry to the left margin; indent subsequent lines 0.5 inches (hanging indentation).
- Alphabetize by the last names of authors; use the last name and first initial (and second initial, if you have it).
- If there are 20 or fewer authors, list all authors. (Use "et al." in the text, but do not use "et al." in the reference list).
- For 21 or more authors, include the names of the first 19 authors, insert an ellipsis, and then add the final author's name.
- Separate authors' names with a comma; however, before the last author listed, use a comma and an ampersand (e.g., Jones, J. D., & Smith, R.).
- If you cite multiple articles by the same author, list the oldest article first, using letters to differentiate the articles.

McGregor, S. A. (2018a)
McGregor, S. A. (2018b, June 30)
McGregor, S. A. (2018c, October 10)

- APA does not use "ibid." (Latin for "in the same source") or "op. cit." (Latin for "in the work already cited") and makes no reference of these terms in their publication manual.
- If there is no author name, list by title, date, then source.
- When the author and the publisher are the same, omit the publisher from the reference.
- Italicize titles of books, and use sentence case (i.e., capitalize only the first word of titles, the first word after a colon, and proper nouns).
- Italicize the titles of journals (including the volume number); use title case for the titles of journals (i.e., capitalize the first letter of major words and prepositions of four or more letters).
- Present the title of journal articles in sentence case.
- If a DOI is available, the "retrieved from" date is not necessary. Provide a retrieval date when citing work that is not archived or is likely to change. (APA, 2020a)

Once again, for greater detail, refer to the *Publication Manual of the American Psychological Association,* 7th ed., visit www.apastyle.apa.org, or use one of the many excellent resources online.

Voice and Plagiarism

Obviously, when you quote or paraphrase information, you need to cite it. However, a "paraphrase" that is the same as the original with only a few changes in wording is not paraphrase; it is plagiarism. In fact, many instructors screen for plagiarism before they even read an assignment. With only a sentence or two, the real source can be identified instantly.

Academic writing can be intimidating. Some writers think they need to sound smart, so their writing becomes pretentious and filled with unnecessarily complicated words and jargon or long, complex sentences. Readers—even academics—are more concerned about quality of thought than complicated wording designed to impress. Thus, one measure of all writing is authenticity.

Until you gain confidence, the words of another will often sound more appealing than your own. However, don't use that as an argument to justify taking parts of someone else's writing. When writers depend on the words of others, rather than their own, they are robbing themselves of skill development and self-confidence. As you write, you are developing your critical thinking skills—your ability to solve problems. Plagiarism interrupts that process, and it also has other long-term repercussions that seem subtle but are no less devastating.

Plagiarism is a form of lying, and research shows that "telling small lies causes changes in the brain that lead people down a 'slippery slope' towards increasingly large acts of dishonesty" (Garrett et al., 2016). In fact, "deceivers often recall how small acts of dishonesty snowballed over time and they suddenly found themselves committing quite large crimes." In effect, each new deception becomes easier than the previous one.

Finding your own voice takes commitment and hard work. Use the following strategies to stay on track:

- Even when you take notes, put ideas in your own words, keeping track of sources for citations.
- When you compose, close your notebook, and write from your own understanding.

You can never expect your writing to be perfect. The value of writing comes from its power as a learning tool. As you write about a topic, you are developing your thinking and ability to solve problems. Learning can be frustrating, and even painful, at times, and there are no shortcuts. Just like writing, learning is a process that takes time. As John Dewey once said, "You become what you learn."

Recap

Each time you use APA style, your skills will improve, and the process will seem easier. However, the *Publication Manual of the American Psychological Association* is a reference manual, and you are not expected to memorize all of its details; make it your goal to learn how to look up specific details by using the index at the back of the book. Also use APA's website, www.apastyle.apa.org, where you will find instructional videos and helpful web pages. In addition, many other excellent resources are available online to support you in getting APA right, improving your confidence and credibility.

WRITING WORKSHOP

Managing Your Writing Process

Instructions: In a small group or with a partner, explore the following, jotting down key points.

1. What is difficult about writing?
   a. What challenges you? For example, do you find getting started or getting organized particularly challenging? What about grammar, punctuation, conciseness? What else challenges you?
   b. Do you edit your writing as you compose?
   c. What changes can you make to improve your writing process?
2. What is difficult about APA style?
   a. What are some of your challenges using APA style? For example, do you find citing sources or formatting your paper particularly challenging? What else challenges you?
   b. What did you learn about APA style in this chapter that you can apply?

Compose Freely—Edit Ruthlessly

The key to good writing is effective editing, and the first step is to stop editing as you compose.

To start, gain insight into how you currently approach a writing task, for example:

- Do you try to figure things out in your head *before* putting words on the page?
- Do you correct grammar, punctuation, and word usage *as you compose*?

FIGURE 1.1   **Managing Your Writing Process**

- Do your ideas dissolve before you get them down?
- Do you submit work without proofreading and editing it?

If you answered *yes* to any of the above questions, you are likely to have *editor's block*:

- **Editor's Block Type A:** You edit as you compose, and your ideas get jammed in your head or dissolve before they reach the page.

- **Editor's Block Type B:** You do not proofread or edit your work because you feel anxious about finding errors or are unsure of what to correct or revise.

You can overcome **Editor's Block Type A** by separating composing from editing: *write freely and then edit ruthlessly.* By writing freely, you will see an immediate difference in your writing, producing more in less time.

You can overcome **Editor's Block Type B** by planning time to edit: set an *internal due date* for your first draft so that you have time for a *final copy edit.*

Work systematically to build your editing skills: each chapter in this book contains principles to apply when you edit. As you build your editing skills, you will see that your voice becomes clear, concise, and engaging.

FIGURE 1.1   **Managing Your Writing Process** *(Continued)*

References

American Psychological Association. (2020a). *Concise guide to APA Style* (7th ed.). https://doi.org/10.1037/0000173-000

American Psychological Association. (2020b). *Publication manual of the American Psychological Association* (7th ed.). American Psychological Association. https://doi.org/10.1037/0000165-000

Garrett, N., Lazzaro, S. C., Ariela, D., & Sharot, T. (2016). The brain adapts to dishonesty. *Nature Neuroscience, 19,* 1727–1732. https://doi.org/10.1038/nn.4426

Lundsford, A., & Connors, R. (2001). *The new St. Martin's handbook.* Bedford/St. Martin's Press.

Schultz, J. (2019, December 3). *APA – The most popular citation style in the world?* Citivi. https://www.citavi.com/en/planned-accidents/articles/apa-the-most-popular-citation-style-in-the-world#:~:text=The%20APA%20citation%20style%20just, total%20of%2015%20million%20copies

University of Manchester. (n.d.). *Academic phrasebank.* Retrieved August 3, 2022, from http://www.phrasebank.manchester.ac.uk/

Author Note: N. Casas, Assistant Librarian for Teaching and Learning, Indiana University, Northwest, contributed to this chapter.

2

FORMATTING

Credibility at a Glance

Though you may spend extraordinary efforts crafting your message, your work is incomplete until you address its most obvious and visible feature: formatting. APA formatting is unique and has specific requirements for spacing, margins and indentation, headings, and font style as well as for the title page, reference page, and quotations. When your paper is formatted correctly, all parts work together harmoniously in a style that satisfies readers' expectations.

Formatting is an element of voice that speaks to your audience, affecting the credibility of a document at a glance. When documents are formatted correctly, readers can focus full attention on content rather than form. In addition, when done well, formatting is a form of visual persuasion, aiding the reader in understanding the content through visual cues. Formatting tools include the use of headings, bullet points and numbering, boldface, and italics. However, the most important element may be the unused portions of the page, or white space.

Formatting documents correctly shows respect for readers and aids in developing good rapport. In fact, each piece of writing you produce—whether that be an academic paper or a professional e-mail—has formatting guidelines. As you develop expert skills, formatting will become an element of your writing style for all documents.

Since formatting is critical and APA style is unique, this chapter contains some built-in redundancy. For example, in the first part of the chapter, some of the same elements of formatting are also explained and illustrated in the second part of the chapter. If you read through this entire chapter, redundancy and all, APA formatting will no longer seem like a mystery.

When you complete this chapter, you will

- know the basics for formatting each part of an APA paper,
- be able to use elements of formatting to create visual cues for the reader,
- understand how formatting affects the reader's expectations and understanding,
- be able to use special features, such as font, color, bold, and italics, as appropriate, and
- be able to format an e-mail message for professional use.

Formatting an APA Paper

Each time you format a paper in APA style, formatting will become easier. However, as previously mentioned, even if you have formatted several papers in the past, don't assume that you understand APA formatting. As a professor once shared, some students complain when points are deducted for obvious formatting errors, insisting other professors have never "criticized" their formatting.

Spacing

Refer to the following spacing guidelines when formatting your APA-style paper:

- Double space your entire paper, including the title page and the reference page. The only exception to this rule is on one area of the title page: add an extra double space after your name.
- Throughout your paper, indent paragraphs 0.5 inches.
- However, do not indent the first line of the abstract.
- On the reference page, use hanging indentation style; align the first line of each reference to the left margin, and indent subsequent lines 0.5 inches.
- Insert one space after a period (APA 6th edition required two spaces after a period).

To set indentation correctly for Microsoft Word, adjust the settings in the Paragraph tab on your toolbar. For example, 0.5 inches is not the same as hitting the space bar 5 times (as would be the case on a typewriter).

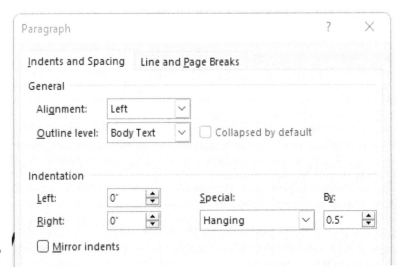

Image 2.1

Settings for the Body of the Document: Paragraph Indentation 0.5"

Image 2.2

Settings for the Reference Page: Hanging Indentation Style

Page Layout and Paragraph Settings

You may choose to adjust your settings while you are writing your draft or when you are making your final edits. Start by setting your margins and paragraph settings for paragraph indentation. Here's how to set margins:

1. Start by setting the paper size to 8.5 inches by 11 inches.
   a. Open the Layout tab.
   b. Click on Size.
   c. Select the Letter option, which is displayed as 8.5" × 11".

2. Set your margins at 1-inch for top, bottom, and sides.
   a. Go to the Layout tab.
   b. Click on Margins, and select Normal.

3. Set your spacing controls for double spacing.
   a. In the Home tab, open the Paragraph window by clicking on the arrow.
   b. In the Indents and Spacing tab, find the Spacing section, and set Before and After to 0 pt.
   c. Set Line Spacing to Double.

4. Set the paragraph indentation for the body of your paper.
   a. With the Paragraph tab open, under Special, select First Line.
   b. Set By at 0.5".
   c. Leave Left and Right at 0".

5. When you are ready to type the reference page, change to hanging indentation style.
   a. With the Paragraph tab open, under Special select Hanging.
   b. Set By at 0.5".

6. Also, keep your right margin uneven.
   a. Select *Align Text Left*; in other words, do not select Justify.

Paragraph ? ✕

Indents and Spacing   Line and Page Breaks

General

Alignment: Left ⌄

Outline level: Body Text ⌄   ☐ Collapsed by default

Indentation

Left: 0"   ⤢

Right: 0"   ⤢

Special: First line ⌄   By: 0.5"   ⤢

☐ Mirror indents

Spacing

Before: 0 pt   ⤢

After: 0 pt   ⤢

Line spacing: Double ⌄   At: ⤢

☐ Don't add space between paragraphs of the same style

Preview

Sample Text Sample Text

Tabs...   Set As Default   OK   Cancel

Image 2.3

Image 2.4

Paragraph

If your paragraph settings for Before and After are not set at 0, parts of your paper will not be double spaced; each time you hit Enter, extra space will appear. Once again, readers trained in APA style will see those errors at a glance.

Headers and Page Numbers

APA requires papers submitted for publication to include a header on each page; however, for student papers, a header only needs to be included when a professor requires it. For both types of submissions, all pages, including the title page and reference page, need to be numbered in the upper-right corner.

In the header, the title can be no longer than 55 characters and may be an abbreviated version of the full title. Notice in the following image that the title of the paper is in all caps at the left margin and the page number is at the right margin.

WRITING A RESEARCH PAPER   1

Image 2.5

Here is one way to insert a page number and title in a header:

1. To open the header, go to the top of the page, and double click.
2. Set Header from Top to 0.5".

Image 2.6

3. Confirm that Different Odd & Even Pages is not selected.

4. Open the Insert tab, and find Page Number.
5. Select Top of Page, and then select the plain number in the upper-right of the page.

Image 2.7

6. To add the title, move the cursor to the left of the page number, and type the header title in all caps. Notice that the cursor is between the page number and title.

Image 2.8

7. With the cursor between the page number and title, hit the Tab key (or space bar) until the title is at the left margin. (If you add too many spaces, the page number will go to the next line; to correct this, delete the extra space.)
8. Check to make sure you are using the same font for your running head and page number as you are for the body of your paper.

Note that if you type the title in the header before you insert page numbers, the title will disappear, and you will need to retype it.

Title Page

On the title page, position title information on the upper third of the page. Double space the title page; however, add an extra double space after the title, which is displayed as a level-1 heading. The following is the template for a student paper:

Title of Paper

Your Name

Date

Course

Instructor

Due Date

Headings

APA uses five levels of headings to differentiate the importance of topics in a similar manner as an outline (see Figure 2.1). For the introduction of your paper, use the title of your paper, formatted as a level-1 heading. In fact, for each section heading use a level-1 heading. Section headings include the title on the title page and the headings for the abstract, introduction, and reference page. For all headings use title case; however, on the reference page, use sentence case (see Chapter 12 for more information).

Level 1 Heading
(centered, bold)
Level 2 Heading
(left, bold—text starts on next line; indent first line of paragraph 0.5")
Level 3 Heading
(left, bold, italics—text starts on next line; indent first line)
Level 4 Heading. [text begins] *(indented, bold)*
Level 5 Heading. [text begins] *(indented, bold, italics)*

FIGURE 2.1   **APA's Five Levels of Headings**

Font Style, Size, and Color

APA aims for consistency and uniformity: the same font and size are used throughout the entire paper, including the title page. In other words, don't try to impress your professor by using a colorful graphic on your cover page or a large-sized font and color; your paper will stand out, but not in the way that you had hoped.

Once again, use only one style font throughout your entire APA paper. Table 2.1 shows the recommended font styles and sizes.

TABLE 2.1 **APA Font Styles**

Serif Font Styles	Sans-Serif Font Style
12-point Times New Roman	11-point Calibri
11-point Georgia	11-point Arial
10-point Computer Modern	10-point Lucinda Sans Unicode

Serif fonts are different from sans-serif fonts in that they have "fancy edges," while sans-serif fonts have "clean edges." In general, when you are writing online, sans serif fonts are easier to read, and when you are writing for print, serif fonts are easier to read.

The only color that should be used is black, including for headings. However, if you use a Word template, your headings may appear in blue, so if you use a template, make sure to change the color to black, and correct the heading styles manually to conform to APA requirements.

- For professional documents, select conservative fonts, and keep them to traditional sizes (no larger than 12 points). Common fonts are Times New Roman for print material and Arial for electronic communication.
- For e-mail messages, if you know your reader has visual difficulty, use a sans-serif font, and increase the font size; you may also use bold formatting to make the message especially clear.

In fact, for e-mail communication, feel free to use the same font size and style as the person with whom you are communicating. In other words, if someone writes to you with a size 14 font, you may respond in like manner, adjusting your style to the other's preference.

Bullet Points and Numbering

Here is how APA (2020) recommends using bullet points and numbering:

- Use numbering for sentences or paragraphs displayed in a series.
  - For items with different degrees of value, use numbers, and list the most important items first.
  - Use the numbered list function, so second lines are automatically indented.
  - Select the style that displays Arabic numbers followed by a period (not a parenthesis).
  - Start the first word of each numbered item (or sentence) with a capital letter, and end it with a period.
- Use bulleted lists for items of equal importance or in which order of priority would not be implied.
  - If the items are phrases, use a bulleted list or letters.
  - For complete sentences, capitalize the first word, and end with a period.
  - For phrases or incomplete sentences, start with a lowercase letter, and do not end with a period.

For bullets, you have a variety of different styles from which to choose. However, stay consistent with the bullet style throughout your document; even for documents that are not formatted in APA style, shift from one style to another only if you have a special purpose for changing styles. For example, you may need to use larger bullets for major points and smaller bullets for minor points.

When you include bulleted lists, display them in parallel structure (e.g., noun for noun, verb for verb, phrase for phrase, and sentence for sentence). For example, if you start with a complete sentence, every item in the list should be displayed as a complete sentence. We'll cover this topic in greater depth in Chapter 11.

In APA style, as well as other styles, when you display items as complete sentences, capitalize the first word, and end with a period, for example:

Some points to consider are as follows:

- Elderly patients are more likely to go untreated because symptoms are not obvious.

- Effective treatment can be tailored to the individual.
- Individuals benefit from a variety of treatments, alone or combined.

When bulleted lists consist of words, phrases, or sentence fragments, APA recommends two options—one ending with punctuation and the other ending without. For both options, start each item with a lowercase letter. Experiment using bullet points and numbering, until you feel comfortable using them.

Short Phrases Option One

For lists of words or short phrases, you do not need to use end punctuation (and this is the preferred method for those types of lists, for example:).

Treatments to address depression in elderly patients include the following:

- art therapy
- physical activity
- music therapy

Short Phrases Option Two

For complicated lists of phrases and incomplete sentences, you can use end punctuation:

Elderly patients with depression often express their need to

- participate in group therapy with others who have similar symptoms,
- become involved in a creative interest that helps them express their feelings, and
- spend time with family and friends off campus. (Jones et al., 2016).

Formatting Features and Marks

Formatting features include bold, underline, and italics; special marks include parentheses and quotation marks. You probably understand not to use all capitals (aka all caps) to stress words or phrases, as all caps connotes shouting. Instead, use syntax to provide emphasis; avoid using italics to stress words in APA style, except when material may be misread. In general writing, you can use italics as well as bold more frequently to stress words.

The following list discusses when different formatting features and marks are appropriate in APA style:

- **bold**
  - Use boldface for all five levels of headings.
  - In professional writing, put words or key ideas in boldface type to make them stand out.
  - Boldface is recommended for short phrases at the beginning of a bullet point.
- **brackets**
  - Enclose material in brackets that is inserted in a quotation by a person other than the original writer.
  - Use brackets to enclose parenthetical material that is already within parentheses.
- **italics**
  - When essential to meaning, use italics to emphasize important words and phrases.
  - Italicize the title of a periodical, book, brochure, or report.
  - Use italics to for the first instance of a key term or phrase for which you will usually provide a definition.
- **quotation marks**
  - Enclose direct quotes and technical terms presented for the first time in quotation marks, using double quotation marks (""); use single quotation marks (') only for quoted material within a quotation.
  - As of APA 7th edition, do not use italics to refer to words as linguistic examples; instead, use quotation marks to refer to a letter, word, phrase, or sentence as a linguistic example or as itself (2020). Use quotation marks in the following examples:
    - The singular pronoun "they" is now preferred.
    - The word "listen" has many shades of meaning.
- **parentheses**
  - Put parentheses around information that gives a brief explanation or that does not directly relate to your topic.

- ○ Enclose abbreviations in parentheses.
- ○ Use parentheses for parenthetical in-text citations.
- **all caps**
  - ○ Follow traditional capitalization guidelines; do not use all caps to make words stand out.
  - ○ Use all caps for the title of your paper in the header.
- **underlining**
  - ○ Underlining is not a formatting tool used in APA style.
  - ○ When you are writing by hand, stress keywords by underlining them.
  - ○ When you are writing by hand, underline the title of a periodical, book, brochure, or report.

Many writers think putting a word between quotation marks makes the idea stand out (e.g., It's a really "good" idea). Instead, when quotation marks are used for no valid reason, readers think that the writer is implying the opposite of what the word actually means. Another mistake writers make is using single quotation marks for reasons other than quoting material within a quotation. Single quotation marks should not be used in place of double quotation marks; for best results, follow the rules (see Figure 2.2).

Recap

Even if your first attempts at citation are not completely correct, your skills will become better with practice. A key element of citation is detail, but do not expect to remember all of the details. When you are unsure, do not guess—when in doubt, check it out.

Now that you know the basics of APA citation style, you can readily use online journal databases that provide APA citation formats. You can find a wealth of information online, including sites that format references in APA style free of charge. However, make sure the site has been updated for the 7th edition of APA. Free tutorials are also available online, including several created by the American Psychological Association (see https://apastyle.apa.org/). The more you work with APA style, the easier it becomes.

QUICK GUIDE TO APA STYLE   1

[Title page: Article for Publication]

Quick Guide to

American Psychological Association (APA) Citation Style

[Authors]

[Affiliations]

Author Note

An author's note is used for articles for publication and would

include each author's departmental and institutional affiliations,

contact information, acknowledgments, disclaimers, and financial

support. However, an author's note would generally not be used

for student assignments, even for theses and dissertations. If you

include an *author's note*, place it on the bottom half of the title

page, as demonstrated here.

FIGURE 2.2   Quick Guide to APA Style

1

[*Title Page: Student Paper*]

Quick Guide to

American Psychological Association (APA) Citation Style

Dina Studentessa

[Affiliation]

[Course]

[Instructor]

[Due Date]

Note: For the title, use title case and position your information on the

upper third of the page.

FIGURE 2.2   Quick Guide to APA Style (*Continued*)

QUICK GUIDE TO APA STYLE   2

Abstract   [*Level Heading 1*]

An abstract is required for articles submitted for publication, but

not required for academic assignments (unless your professor

makes it part of the assignment). An abstract is a one-paragraph

summary no longer than 250 words summarizing the key ideas

of the work. (Note that an abstract is *not* the introduction.) For

published papers, a well-written abstract and keyword summary

are critical for the paper to show up in relevant searches. Place

the abstract on the second page, right after the title page. The

title "abstract" is formatted as a level 1 heading, which is why it

is centered and in boldface. Also, though paragraphs throughout

your paper are indented one-half inch, *do not indent the first line*

of your abstract. The *keyword summary* appears a double space

below the abstract: "Keywords" is in italics and indented 0.5

inches.

        Keywords: APA style, APA formatting, running head, APA

example, APA title page, abstract

FIGURE 2.2   Quick Guide to APA Style (*Continued*)

QUICK GUIDE TO APA STYLE   3

Quick Guide to APA Citation Style   [Level 1 Heading]

This guide illustrates common elements of APA style, providing

some formatting guidelines. However, when you have a detailed

question about style or citation format, consult the *Publication*

Manual of the American Psychological Association (2020) or visit

the APA's website at www.apastyle.apa.org.

To start, articles for publication have some formatting

differences from student assignments. For example, articles for

publication require a *running head* and an *abstract*; which are both

illustrated in this brief guide. However, for student assignments,

include the running head and abstract only if your professor

requires them. Student papers include these parts: *title page,*

introduction, main body, and *references*. If you include an abstract,

start it on a new page; also start your references on a new page.

If you are *not* including an abstract, start your introduction

on page 2. Rather than titling it "introduction," use the title of

your paper for the introduction. Use level 1 heading, which is in

boldface and centered. In your introduction, discuss the problem

and its importance as well as your process or research strategy,

FIGURE 2.2   Quick Guide to APA Style (*Continued*)

QUICK GUIDE TO APA STYLE   4

presenting your thesis or hypothesis. Start the body of your paper

below your introduction on the same page.

Formatting   *[Level 1 Heading]*

Formatting is a critical element of your paper: formatting

is itself a code to the reader. Readers can see *at a glance* if your

work is formatted correctly, and documents that are formatted

according to the guidelines gain credibility. Thus, take the time to

set your paragraph and spacing controls.

Your entire paper should be double spaced on a page sized at

8.5" by 11" (letter size) with 1-inch top, bottom, and side margins

(which is often the default setting, but not always). Note that

while all parts of your paper should be double spaced, add an extra

double space after the title on the title page. Space one time after

all punctuation marks including the period.

For the body of your paper, indent the first line of each

paragraph 0.5 inches (one-half inch) and use *align left*: your right

margins should be uneven (as shown here). For your spacing

to be correct, paragraph controls need to be set consistently

throughout your entire document. Thus, if you are formatting

FIGURE 2.2   Quick Guide to APA Style (*Continued*)

QUICK GUIDE TO APA STYLE 5

a draft, use the Select All function (at Home page, click on "Editing" tab, then click on "Select," choosing "Select All"). After you click on "Select All," set paragraph controls. Under "Spacing," set "Before" and "After" at 0. Under "Linespacing," select "Double."

Use the same font and size throughout your entire paper, including the header, page numbers, title page and references.

Formatting Features and Marks   [*Level 2 Heading*]

The formatting features and marks you will use most frequently are quotation marks, italics, and parentheses.

Quotation Marks [*Level 3 Heading*]

1. Enclose a direct quote of fewer than 40 words within the body of a document.

2. Identify jargon or coined expressions that may be unfamiliar.

3. Use words humorously or ironically.

4. Show a slang expression, poor grammar, or an intentionally misspelled word.

FIGURE 2.2   Quick Guide to APA Style (*Continued*)

QUICK GUIDE TO APA STYLE   6

Italics

1.   Emphasize a word, phrase, or entire sentence.

2.   Display book titles and journal titles.

3.   Identify a word or phrase as a linguistic example.

Parentheses

1.   Include a brief explanation within a sentence.

2.   Insert a sentence that does not directly relate to the topic of

     your paragraph.

3.   Supply abbreviations.

Using parentheses tells the reader that the information relates

to the broader topic without going into detail of how or why.

Thus, you can sometimes avoid writing a lengthy explanation by

enclosing a few words in parentheses.

Page Numbering and Running Head   [*Level 2 Heading*]

     Starting with the title page, number all pages, with the

number appearing in the upper-right corner at the right margin.

If you are submitting an article for publication, your document

also needs a running head; however, if you are submitting an

FIGURE 2.2   Quick Guide to APA Style (*Continued*)

QUICK GUIDE TO APA STYLE   7

assignment for one of your classes, include a running head only if

your instructor requires it. Insert numbering first, and then insert

the running head.

Your title in your header should be flush with the left margin,

and the page number should appear at the right margin.

Headings and Subheadings   [*Level 2 Heading*]

APA guidelines provide five levels of headings. Table 2.2 on

page 8 below displays the various headings, describing whether

each is centered, blocked at the left, or indented as well as whether

each is presented in boldface type or italics. Note that levels 4

and 5 are paragraph headings, with text starting on the same line

following the period.

Charts and Graphs   [*Level 2 Heading*]

APA allows charts and graphs to be integrated into the

body of the paper or placed on a separate page at the end of the

document, following the reference page. Below is a table for the

five levels of headings, integrated into this paper. Notice that

the graph appears on the next page because it would not fit in its

entirety on this page.

FIGURE 2.2   Quick Guide to APA Style (*Continued*)

QUICK GUIDE TO APA STYLE 8

Table 2.2   Five Levels of Headings

Level 1 Heading (*centered, boldface*)
Level 2 Heading (*left, boldface—start text on the next line, indented*)
Level 3 Heading (*left, boldface, italics—start text on the next line, indented*)
Level 4 Heading. [text begins] (*indented, boldface*)
Level 5 Heading. [text begins] (*indented, boldface, italicized*)

Type the following using level 1 heading: title of your paper, title of your introduction (use the title of your paper), abstract, and reference or references.

In-Text Citation   *[Level 1 Heading]*

Use the author-date citation system to identify your sources, crediting authors whether you quote them directly or put their ideas and research in your own words. For indirect references or paraphrased statements, use a *narrative citation*, citing the author's last name and the publication year in parentheses as part of the sentence:

Narrative citation: Greger (2018) included nutrition facts identified through recent research.

FIGURE 2.2   Quick Guide to APA Style (*Continued*)

QUICK GUIDE TO APA STYLE   9

For direct quotes, include the page number (or paragraph

number if there is no page number) as a *parenthetical citation* (in

parentheses at the end of the quotation). However, if you use the

author's name and date in your text, do not repeat the author's

name at the end of the sentence:

    Parenthetical citation: "All students can learn what the schools

                    teach if they can find an interest in it."

                    (Tyler, 1988, p. 45)

    Narrative citation: Tyler (1988) stated, "All students can

                    learn what the schools teach if they can

                    find an interest in it" (p. 45).

For a citation that has only one author, list the author's last name

and the year of the publication. For a citation with two authors, list

both authors for all citations; for example:

    Narrative citation: Barnard and Klaper (2019) provided

                    evidence to support nutrition-based

                    eating.

For citations with three or more authors, use et al. (the Latin

abbreviation for "and others"), for example:

FIGURE 2.2   Quick Guide to APA Style *(Continued)*

QUICK GUIDE TO APA STYLE   10

    Narrative citation: McDougal et al. (2001) supported

                         their thesis with data from previous

                         research.

For narrative citations, use the word "and"; for parenthetical

citations, use the ampersand (&). And once again, for complex

citations, check the APA publication manual.

               Grammar: The Singular "They"   [*Level 1 Heading*]

    In its 7th edition, the publication manual of the APA shifted

to the use of gender-neutral pronouns, requiring the use of the

singular "they," when needed. As a result, APA style no longer

accepts the use of "he" or "she" or their related forms ("his/her,"

and so on). Thus, in place of third-person singular pronouns,

writers would use the singular "they" or edit out the need for a

pronoun (such as making antecedents plural).

    When referring to a person of unknown gender identity,

refer to the person by name. While this may become redundant,

redundancy is preferred to being offensive. Also, when a person

asks to be referred to in a specified way, respect the request,

even if the reference is unfamiliar or nontraditional.

FIGURE 2.2   Quick Guide to APA Style (*Continued*)

QUICK GUIDE TO APA STYLE   11

Word Usage: Unbiased Language   *[Level 1 Heading]*

For the sake of accuracy and diversity, choose words

that eliminate bias from writing and speech. The American

Psychological Association along with other sources give specific

language guidelines. For example, here is information from the

"Press Guidelines for Describing People" (NASW, 2020):

1. Seek out and use the preference of the people about whom

    you write.

2. Be specific about age, race, and culture.

3. Describe people in the positive by stating what they are rather

    than what they are not.

4. Refer to a disability or specify sex only when it is relevant.

5. Use people-first language unless a person has indicated

    another preference.

Reference Page   *[Level 1 Heading]*

Place the reference list at the end of the paper on a separate

page using double spacing (every part of an APA paper is double

spaced). For references, list only those works that you cite in the

text. Arrange the citations in alphabetical order by last name for

FIGURE 2.2   **Quick Guide to APA Style** (*Continued*)

QUICK GUIDE TO APA STYLE   12

works that have an author. If there is no author, list by title, date,

and source.

Each reference with an author would include the following:

the last names and initials of authors (first names are not used in

APA style), publication date, title of work, and publisher as well

as DOIs (digital object identifiers) and URLs (uniform resource

locators), when applicable.

Title the first page of your reference list using a level 1

heading with the word "Reference" or "References." For each

reference, block the first line at the left margin and then use

hanging indentation style for second lines, indenting second lines

0.5 inches.

Each type of reference requires a specific format: refer

directly to the formatting guidelines for the type of source that

you are citing, such as books, journal articles, websites, and so on.

In fact, in addition to the APA publication manual, you may also

want to experiment using a citation generator. To find one, search

for "citation generator apa."

FIGURE 2.2   **Quick Guide to APA Style** (*Continued*)

QUICK GUIDE TO APA STYLE   13

Resources   *[Level 1 Heading]*

Doing anything new for the first time is difficult. After you have formatted your first few assignments in APA citation style, you will feel more confident. Also, keep your resources close at hand so that you can check and then double check whenever you have a doubt or a question.

Writing Tip

Page Breaks

When you write a paper, keep at least two lines of content on the same page as the heading.

- Do not put a heading at the bottom of one page with the narrative starting on the next page. (Bring the heading to the fresh page.)

If you are at the end of a page and need to break up a paragraph, keep at least two lines on each page. For example, if a paragraph is only three lines long, move the three-line paragraph to the top of the next page.

Writing Tip

And & the Ampersand

For *narrative citations*, use the word *and*; for *parenthetical citations* at the end of a sentence, use the ampersand (&).

Jones and Smith (2018) agree that research is important.

Research is important (Smith & Jones, 2019).

For your *reference list*, use the ampersand:

Jones, R., & Smith, C. (2018). *Research is important: Do your research now.* Action Research Publishers.

FIGURE 2.2   Quick Guide to APA Style (*Continued*)

QUICK GUIDE TO APA STYLE   14

References   *[Level 1 Heading]*

American Psychological Association. (2020). *Publication manual*

of the American Psychological Association. (7th ed.). https://

doi.org/10.1037/0000165-000

National Association for Social Workers. (2020). NASW press

guidelines for describing people. http://www.pear.org/resource/

nasw-press-guidelines-for-describing-people

Writing Tip

Primary and Secondary Sources

Primary sources report original content, but secondary sources refer to content first reported in another source. To start, use secondary sources *only* when the original source is not available or accessible—when possible, go to the original source.

Here's how to use a secondary source:

1. *For parenthetical citations*, identify the primary source and then write "as cited in" the secondary source. Also include the year of publication of the primary source, if known, for example:

   (Jones, 1989, as cited in Smithe et al., 2019)

2. *For narrative citations*, if the year of the primary source is not known, omit it from the in-text citation:

   Jones' research (as cited in Smithe et al., 2019) revealed that …

3. *On the reference page*, include only the secondary source.

FIGURE 2.2   Quick Guide to APA Style (*Continued*)

WRITING WORKSHOP

Writing a Process Message

Instructions: Write a process message for your professor, discussing what you learned in this chapter.

1. Identify four or more key points that stood out for you about APA style.

2. Format your process message by using a greeting and closing.

3. Give your professor an update about any projects you are currently working on.

FIGURE 2.3   **Writing a Process Message**

In a process message, you can discuss your learning process by sharing insights, asking questions, and giving updates. Think of a *process* message as a *progress* message. (Your professor will pro-vide details about how to send your message.)

APA 7th Edition Checklist

Student Papers

- title page
  - page number (upper right)
  - paper title (follow with extra double space)
  - author (or authors)
  - affiliation

    course

    instructor

    due date
- abstract (optional)
- main body
  - level-1 heading (centered, bold)
  - level-2 heading (left, bold)
  - level-3 heading (left, bold, italics)
  - level-4 heading (body text indented, bold)
  - level-5 heading (body text indented, bold, italics)
- references

Articles for Publication

- title page
  - title (left) and page number (right)

(title in header 50 characters or less)

  - paper title (follow with an extra double space)
  - author or authors
  - affiliation(s)
  - author note
- abstract
- main body
  - introduction (use title of paper)

- o methods
- o results
- o discussion
- o conclusion
- references

Formatting

- Use 1-inch margins; leave the right margin uneven.
- Double space the entire document; indent the first line of each paragraph 0.5 inches.
- On the title page, center the title and bylines on the upper half of the page.
- Begin numbering on the title page.
- Insert one space after punctuation marks, including periods.
- Choose one of the following font styles, and use it throughout:
  - o 12-point Times New Roman
  - o 11-point Georgia
  - o 10-point Computer Modern
  - o 11-point Calibri
  - o 11-point Arial
  - o 10-point Lucinda Sans Unicode

Titles

- **title case:** Capitalize all major words; use on the title page, in the text, and for all headings.
- **sentence case:** Capitalize only the first word, the first word after a colon, and proper nouns; use for book and article titles on the reference page.

Quotations

- For quotations of 40 words or more, use block quotes. Double space and indent 0.5 inches from the left margin; do not use quotation marks, and put the reference outside the period.
- For short quotations, put the citation inside the period.

Abstract

- Develop a synopsis of your paper in one paragraph no longer than 250 words (required for articles for publication).
- Do not indent the first line.
- Include a keyword summary after the abstract, indenting and italicizing keywords.

Body

- Indent paragraphs 0.5 inches.
- Leave right margins uneven (align left; do not justify).
- Use headings as needed. If one level of heading is needed, use level 1; if two are needed, use levels 1 and 2; and so on.
- Integrate short visuals (e.g., tables, graphs, or charts) into the text of your paper.
- Place large visuals on separate pages at the end of your paper or in an appendix.

In-Text Citations

- For narrative and parenthetical citations, use the last names of authors and the year of publication.

  Jones (2019) found that at-risk youth needed additional support.

  At-risk youth were likely to have issues with self-esteem (Jones, 2019).

- When a work has two authors, cite both names each time. When a work has three or more authors, use the last name of the first author followed by "et al.":

  According to Jones and Smithe (2015), clients participated.

  Martinez et al. (2018) conducted the study that was cited.

- In subsequent references within the same paragraph, the date is unnecessary.
- For narrative citations, use the word "and." For parenthetical citations at the end of a sentence, use an ampersand.

Reference Page

- List references in alphabetical order, leaving individual references in the order noted in the article or book.
- Use the author's last name and first initial (no first names).
- For books, use the author's last name and initials, publication date, title of work, and publisher.
- Align the first line of each reference to the left margin.
- Indent second lines of references 0.5 inches (i.e., use hanging indentation).
- Present the title of a book in sentence case, the title of an article in sentence case, and the title of a journal in title case.
- Italicize the title of a book, the title of a journal, and a journal's volume number.

Reference

American Psychological Association. (2020). *Publication manual of the American Psychological Association* (7th ed.). American Psychological Association. https://doi.org/10.1037/0000165-000

Figure Credits

3

GENDER-NEUTRAL PRONOUNS, VIEWPOINT, AND VOICE

American Psychological Association (APA) guidelines promote inclusivity, providing writers with tools to avoid bias. One of these tools is the use of gender-neutral pronouns.

Pronouns are a core element of everything you write. For example, each sentence is written from a specific *viewpoint*, such as *first-person* (i.e., "I" and "we"), *second-person* (i.e., "you"), or *third-person* (i.e., "he," "she," "it," "they," and "the researcher") viewpoint. Academic writing relies on the third-person viewpoint; the second-person "you" viewpoint is not used, and only under defined contexts is the first-person "I" viewpoint used.

The third-person singular viewpoint is gender specific; however, in its 7th edition, the *Publication Manual of the American Psychological Association* (2020) shifted to the use of gender-neutral pronouns, requiring the use of the singular "they," when needed:

- APA style no longer accepts the use of "he" or "she" or their related forms, "him," "her," and so on, when referring to a person of unknown gender identity or as generic pronouns.
- In place of third-person singular pronouns, writers would use the singular "they" (or apply other options, as discussed in this chapter) when referring to people of unknown or when gender identity is irrelevant.

When you complete this chapter, you be able to

- apply APA guidelines for pronoun viewpoint, voice, and verb tense,
- avoid gender bias by using the singular "they," cutting the pronoun reference, or making antecedents plural,
- refer to authors by last name and initials, and
- display consistent use of the third-person viewpoint for academic writing.

While this chapter discusses the use of pronouns, Chapter 4 provides additional directives on language usage and APA style.

Pronoun Viewpoint

Pronoun viewpoint refers to the point of view from which a document is written, which can be first, second, or third person and singular or plural. For a quick refresher on pronouns, review Table 3.1.

TABLE 3.1   **Personal Pronouns**

	Subjective	Objective	Possessive	Reflexive
Singular				
1st person	I	me	my mine	myself
2nd person	you	you	your yours	yourself
3rd person	he	him	his	himself
	she	her	hers	herself
	it	it	its	itself
Gender neutral	they	them	their theirs	themselves themself
Plural				
1st person	we	us	our ours	ourselves
2nd person	you	you	you yours	yourselves
3rd person	they	them	their theirs	themselves

Here is the role each case plays in a sentence:

- **Subjective case** pronouns function as *subjects* of verbs, and thus, a subjective case pronoun is used as the subject of a sentence.
- **Objective case** pronouns function as *objects*, usually of verbs or prepositions.
- **Possessive case** pronouns show possession of nouns or other pronouns.
- **Reflexive case** pronouns reflect back to subjective case pronouns; reflexive case pronouns are also known as *intensive case pronouns*.
- **Gender-neutral pronouns** are used in APA style to refer to people in a manner neutral toward gender.

APA Style and Gender-Neutral Pronouns

When pronouns are used, the words they refer to are known as *antecedents*. An antecedent can be singular or plural; when antecedents are singular, traditional grammar may designate that a gender-specific pronoun, such as "he" or "she," be used. However, with APA's exclusion of the use of third-person singular pronouns for people of unknown gender identity, some usage that would have been incorrect in the past may now be correct. Here is an update:

- For singular antecedents such as "person," "psychologist," "researcher," "client," "patient," and so on, APA style, and some other style books, require the use of the singular "they" as a gender-neutral pronoun.
  - APA no longer accepts the use of "he" or "she" (or variations such as "he/she") as gender-neutral, third-person pronouns.
- At the time of writing, citation systems such as Modern Library Association (2020) and the *Chicago Manual of Style* (2017) allow but do not require the use of the singular "they" as a gender-neutral pronoun for singular antecedents.

Since some audiences have not yet fully adopted the use of singular "they," use it sparingly and only when necessary. By using other options (such as the ones discussed below), your writing will remain correct and free of gender bias.

Gender-Neutral Options

To achieve gender neutrality, the following are additional options to using the singular "they":

1. Use the third-person plural.
2. Replace the gender reference with an article, such as "the," "a," or "an."
3. Rephrase the sentence by dropping the pronoun reference.

TABLE 3.2   **Gender-Neutral Options**

Gender Biased	Option	Gender Neutral
A client should contact his or her therapist.	Use the third-person plural.	Clients should contact *their* therapists.
When a researcher conducts her study, research participants must be informed of changes.	Substitute with an article.	When a researcher conducts *a* study, research participants must be informed of changes.
In an emergency, a person must do what he or she is asked.	Drop the pronoun.	In an emergency, a person must do what is asked.

APA and Gender Reference

APA guidelines regarding gender terminology are not only specific but also detailed. Therefore, when you do research or write extensively about gender, refer directly to guidelines outlined in the *Publication Manual of the American Psychological Association*, 7th edition (2020). Here are a few points APA stresses:

- To refer to the pronouns that transgender and gender-nonconforming people use, use the terms "identified pronouns," "self-identified pronouns," or "pronouns." Do not use the term "preferred pronouns."
- Use a person's identified pronouns. Some individuals use "they" as a singular pronoun; some use alternative pronouns, such as "ze," "xe," "hir," "per," "ve," "ey," and "hen."

- Some people alternate between "he" and "she" or between "he and/or she" and "they," whereas others use no pronouns at all, using their name in place of pronouns.
- Avoid using combinations that are exclusively binary, such as "he" or "she," "she or he," "he/she," and "(s)he" as alternatives to the singular "they."
- Refer to a transgender person using language appropriate to that person's gender, regardless of sex assigned at birth.

When you refer to a person and are unaware of the person's gender, refer to the person by name. While this may become redundant, redundancy is preferred to being offensive. (And when feasible, do some research or ask.)

- When a person asks to be referred to in a specific way, respect the request, even if the reference is unfamiliar or nontraditional.

If you have questions about word usage, do more research. Language changes as customs and norms change. By remaining inclusive, you avoid bias, which is a critical element of academic writing.

APA Style and Viewpoint

In addition to using gender-neutral pronouns, APA gives other directives about how to use pronoun viewpoint effectively (2020). Therefore, let us look at the following three pronoun viewpoints and how they fit into your formal academic writing:

- third-person viewpoint
- "I" viewpoint
- "we" viewpoint (aka the "editorial we")

Third-Person Viewpoint

For the most part, the third-person viewpoint is the voice of academic writing.

1. In general, use the third-person viewpoint.

   The *study* produced data that reinforced previous research (Williams, 2018).

   Jones (2020) conducted the research.

   Barnes and Blake (2015) argue that too much time is spent on the Internet.

   The *Internet* distracts learners from tasks that require critical thinking.

2. When referring to the author of a study, book, or article, use the author's last name. If there are two authors with the same last name, include their initials.

   incorrect: Jane's findings were supported by subsequent research.

   correct: Franklin's (2012) findings were supported by subsequent research.

   correct: T. Jackson and F. Jackson (2018) studied addiction in various age groups and how it affects family relationships.

3. Focus on the research and not the researchers conducting it. Therefore, when you summarize a research article, start by stating the author's name, then shift focus to the research itself.

   Barnes (2010) argues that the Internet can divert users from their original objective, causing them to lose time and focus. The *research* specifically identifies students as being at risk for getting sidetracked from academic tasks. *Findings* include data about distracted learners who experience more stress than value from experiences in which they lose focus.

   The *Internet* has many uses, ranging from personal interests to being an academic research vehicle. However, *sites* such as Facebook interfere with student learning and their research on the Internet (Johnson, 2018).

4. When you are the sole author of a paper, do not use the third-person viewpoint. In other words, do not refer to yourself as "the author" or "this researcher."

Since most of your academic writing is in the third-person viewpoint, learn to speak with consistency in that viewpoint. In other words, stay within the third-person viewpoint throughout your entire document, unless you have specific reasons for using the "I" viewpoint. For example, at times, the first-person viewpoint is not only necessary but also desirable; let us review those times.

"I" Viewpoint

In academic writing, use the first-person "I" viewpoint for the following:

* when you are describing research you have conducted alone
* when you express your views, such as when making concluding remarks or stating recommendations

At those times when the "I" viewpoint is appropriate, it is preferred to the passive voice.

Passive: A recommendation is that further research in this area is needed.

"I" viewpoint (preferred): I recommend that further research in this area explore *x*, *y*, and *z*.

To avoid overusing the "I" viewpoint, focus on the research and not yourself.

"I" viewpoint: I found that the amount of time on task is critical.

Third person (preferred): The results of the research indicate that the amount of time on task is critical.

In the body of your work, your aim is to write about topics in an objective way. Thus, if you find yourself using the first-person viewpoint, do a self-check to see if you may be including beliefs or opinions that would be best edited out of your draft.

Finally, use the "I" viewpoint to refer to yourself (rather than using the third-person viewpoint). For example, when you write notes, refer to yourself as "I," not "the psychologist," "the researcher," "the author of this study," and so on.

Third person: This writer found that several issues need to be resolved.

"I" viewpoint (preferred): I found that several issues need to be resolved.

"We" Viewpoint

When you work with others on a project, use the "we" viewpoint rather than referring to yourself and your colleagues in the third person.

Third person: The authors received a grant to cover the cost of resources.

"We" viewpoint (preferred): We received a grant to cover the cost of resources.

When using the pronoun "we," use it in specific ways; for example, do not use the editorial "we," which some writers use to express their opinions.

In other words, use "we" only when you have co-authors—do not use "we" when you are referring only to yourself.

Editorial "we": We need to write in an unbiased way.

Revised: As psychologists, we need to write in an unbiased way.

Editorial "we": We generally cover that information with our clients.

Revised: As therapists, we generally cover that information with our clients.

Academic Viewpoint: Active Voice and Passive Voice

In academic writing, pronouns and verbs work together to construct a viewpoint and voice. For example, to avoid speaking from a personal voice, writers commonly use *passive voice*. (In the passive voice, the grammatical subject does not perform the action of the verb.) Though passive voice is necessary and accepted in academic writing, APA style recommends using the *active voice* when possible. (In the active voice, the grammatical subject is also the real subject and performs the action of the verb.)

Passive voice: Responses were given by the participants for all five parts of the study.

Active voice: Participants gave responses for all five parts of the study.

Passive voice: It was concluded that the research was valid.

Active voice: The authors concluded that the research was valid.

When you write about someone else's work, academic writing requires the third person. For example, when you are summarizing an article, you are not writing from your point of view; you are writing from the viewpoint of the article's author. Let us say you are summarizing an article written by psychologist Carl Rogers. As you discuss Rogers, you would most effectively write from the third-person point of view.

Rogers (1985) argued that every person strives to be self-reliant.

Person-centered therapy was a central focus of Rogers's therapy.

In these examples, the reader is not addressed directly. Instead, the third-person viewpoint focuses on the topic and what the article's author writes about it. Writing from this viewpoint, you would connect to the reader in an indirect way, not a direct way.

Once again, in academic assignments avoid using first-person pronouns, such as "I" and "me," unless the assignment includes a self-reflective component. In academic writing you would not speak directly to your audience, so you would also not use second-person pronouns, such as "you" and "your." For academic assignments in which you present your opinions, such as a literature review, support your opinions with evidence.

Verb Tenses

APA gives specific guidance on when to use past, present, and future tenses as you discuss your research and the research of others:

- **discussing the work of other researchers**

  past tense: Jones (2020) *concluded* the research was flawed.

  present perfect: Other researchers *have presented* similar results.

- **describing methods**

  past tense: Each group *attended* an orientation.

  present perfect: Several other studies *have identified* similar outcomes.

- **reporting results**

  past tense: Participants *increased* in the years following the pandemic.

  past tense: The results *revealed* outcomes that were not expected.

- **discussing implications**

  present tense: Our data *indicate* additional populations need to be included.

- **presenting conclusions, limitations, and future directions**

  present tense: We *find* that that the information is outdated.

  present tense: We suggest that further research *explore* this topic.

  present tense: Limitations of this study *include* lack of research in this area.

- **starting your paper**

  present tense: This paper explores the benefits of play therapy.

Professional Voice

Write from your *professional voice* when you write e-mail messages to professors and colleagues. Limit your use of the "I" viewpoint when using your professional voice, shifting to the "you" viewpoint when possible.

Weak: *I* need your assistance.

Revised: Would *you* be able to assist me?

When you write with your professional voice, connect with readers through simple, clear, concise writing. Therefore, you should use first- and second-person pronouns (e.g., "I," "we," and "you") to speak to your reader in a direct and personal way.

"I" viewpoint: *I* would like to invite you to our next meeting.

"you" viewpoint: Would *you* be interested in attending our next meeting?

"I" viewpoint: *I* would like to know what you think about the change.

"you" viewpoint: What do *you* think about the change?

"I" viewpoint: *I* would like to encourage you to apply for the position.

"you" viewpoint: *You* should apply for the position.

At times, the "I" viewpoint is necessary to avoid writing that is awkward, which is never effective. For professional writing, here's a general approach: *If you wouldn't say it that way, don't write it that way.* Thus, when you are writing about your own experience, use the "I" point of view.

awkward: When the project *was started by me*, a request was made.

"I" viewpoint: When *I* started this project, *I* requested the data.

In business, writers also use the "we" viewpoint, sometimes known as the editorial "we."

editorial "we": *We* at Focus Research Group value your support.

While the "you" viewpoint puts focus on the reader, the "I" viewpoint comes more naturally when composing. Thus, when you compose, let your words flow freely. When you edit, shift to the "you" viewpoint. Compose for yourself, then edit for your reader.

Reflective Voice

Write with your *reflective voice* for personal journals, notes, and blogs. For reflective writing that is personal, write in whatever style you wish. When you are expressing your feelings and opinions, you naturally speak from the "I" viewpoint.

Another purpose of reflective writing is to keep track of events and record your thoughts, at times in a work journal. In fact, in some professions, notes are considered official records. Thus, when you are employed under those circumstances, be fastidious with your personal notes; adjust your voice and writing style for the possibility that they could become part of a legal case and enter the public domain. In other words, writing on the job is a form of legal documentation.

Do you currently write online? This type of reflective writing is already part of the public domain and used by potential employers to screen applicants. Be especially cautious about expressing personal views online. Careers have been destroyed by a single tweet or post; text messages have also destroyed careers and been used as evidence in civil and criminal cases.

Recap

A critical part of all writing is to adapt your voice for your specific audience. Here is a recap of some key points about pronoun usage in academic writing:

- Avoid gender reference by using the singular "they"; however, use the singular "they" sparingly by making antecedents plural or dropping the pronoun reference, when possible.
- To further avoid gender bias, refer to authors by last name.
- For academic writing, do not use the "you" viewpoint.
- Avoid using the "I" viewpoint, unless you are the sole author of a paper.
- Don't refer to yourself in the third person; when you write professional notes, use "I" (not "this author").
- If you coauthor a paper, you and your coauthors may refer to yourselves as "we."
- When you share insights and recommendations in concluding remarks of a paper, you may use the "I" viewpoint.

WRITING WORKSHOP

Pronoun Consistency: Third-Person Plural

Instructions: Edit the following paragraph using the third person plural viewpoint (e.g., "people," they/them, and so on), correcting pronouns for consistency.

example: A new member should review your assignment to find out about one's new projects.

corrected: *New members* should review *their* assignments to find about *their* new projects.

An intern must understand that you will experience a period of adjustment at their new assignment. Unfortunately, many new interns think that one's colleagues should adjust to you instead of the other way around. When you begin a new duty, one should "lay low" for the first few months to learn the way the environment functions. After one has held a position for three or four months, you can begin making appropriate suggestions and changes.

ACTIVITY KEY

Pronoun Consistency: Third-Person Plural

Note: Answers may vary.

~~An intern~~ *Interns* must understand that ~~you~~ *they* will experience a period of adjustment at their new assignment. Unfortunately, many new interns think that ~~one's~~ *their* colleagues should adjust to ~~you~~ *them* instead of the other way around. When ~~you~~ *interns* begin a new duty, ~~one~~ *they* should "lay low" for the first few months to learn the way the environment functions. After ~~one has~~ *they have* held a position for three or four months, ~~you~~ *interns* can begin making appropriate suggestions and changes.

CRITIC'S BLOCK

Another issue that holds writers back is *critic's block*. When you write, you face the unknown, which is always uncomfortable. At those times, push through doubts and fears. Critic's block is exemplified by having a subtle, nagging anxiety about writing. When you think about writing, you remember negative feedback you didn't understand or expect. As a result, you put off writing tasks because the writing process feels uncomfortable and even intimidating.

To overcome critic's block, turn off messages that are self-defeating; no one writes perfectly. In fact, fear of criticism is often worse than criticism itself; that is because once you hear the actual words, you can regroup and emerge stronger. In contrast, fear is paralyzing, and the only way to combat fear is to take action. Start writing, even if you are writing about your own fears.

References

American Psychological Association. (2020). *Publication manual for the American Psychological Association* (7th ed.). https://doi.org/10.1037/0000165-000

Chicago Manual. (April 3, 2017). Chicago style for the singular they. CMOS Shop Talk. https://cmosshoptalk.com/2017/04/03/chicago-style-for-the-singular-they/

MLA Style Center. (March 4, 2020). How do I use singular *they*? https://style.mla.org/using-singular-they/

4

UNBIASED AND GENDER-NEUTRAL LANGUAGE

anguage helps define the way that we perceive the world around us, and the American Psychological Association (APA) takes a strong and decisive position about using words to promote inclusivity and diversity:

> Precision is essential in scholarly writing; when you refer to a person or persons, choose words that are accurate, clear, and free from bias or prejudicial connotations. Bias, like inaccurate or unclear language, can be a form of imprecision. (2020, p. 132)

To support you in producing writing that is correct and precise and that sets an effective tone, this chapter provides some basics for using unbiased language. Included is terminology to discuss race, ethnicity, and gender as well as disability and aging, assisting you in using inclusive terms that respect diversity. However, the information here is only the beginning. When you conduct your own research or construct surveys, refer to the *Publication Manual of the American Psychological Association*, 7th edition for guidance on the fine details of unbiased use of language.

When you complete this chapter, you will be able to

- use unbiased and gender-neutral language in writing and speech, and
- apply effective and specific language when referring to race, ethnicity, and gender as well as disability and aging.

Unbiased and Gender-Neutral Language Guidelines

Word choice creates a picture, setting a tone. For the sake of accuracy and diversity, choose words that eliminate bias from your writing and your speech. The APA along with other sources give specific language guidelines—some of which are discussed in this section. For example, the National Association of Social Workers (NASW) publishes a pamphlet, *Press Guidelines for Describing People* (2022) with guidance on the topic. Here is a summary of some key points:

- **Seek and use the preference of the people that you write about.** However, at times, people will use stigmatizing language to refer to themselves. When that is the case, be cautious about repeating the stigmatizing language, as it could promote the use of the slur and affect others.
- **Be specific about age, race, and culture.** For example, rather than using broad categories, such as "Asian Americans," use specific descriptors, such as "Chinese Americans."
- **Describe people in the positive.** State what people are rather than what they are not.
- **Refer to a disability or specify sex only when it is relevant.** When a category is not a variable in your research or essential to your discussion, do not include it.
- **Use people-first language, unless a person has indicated another preference.** For example, avoid using terms that label people, such as "the disabled"; instead use person-first language, such as "people with disabilities."

These points and others are discussed below. However, language is ever changing, so continue to research and update your understanding. For additional information, do an Internet search on "language guidelines for describing people." For example, one excellent source is the National Center on Disability and Journalism (NCDJ), which also offers a style guide (2021).

Gender-Neutral Language

The American Sociological Association (ASA) gives the following recommendation on gender-neutral language:

> Unless gendered terms are specific to analysis of data or demographics, use nongendered terms such as *person, people, individual,* or *humankind* rather than *man, men,* or *mankind* [sic]. (2014, p. 4)

The Singular "They"

As discussed in Chapter 3, writers using APA style should now use "they" as a generic third-person singular pronoun, when needed. Here are some ways to avoid using gender in writing:

1. Avoid slashed gender terms (e.g., "he/she"), repetition of the conjunction or (e.g., "he or she") and switching gender order (e.g., "he" or "she" and then "she or he," and so on); that is, unless those forms are a person's preference. For writing in general, use the plural form of the noun or pronoun.

   gender specific: When *a person* writes, *he or she* needs to stay on topic.

   gender neutral: When *people* write, *they* need to stay on topic.

2. Replace the pronoun with a nonspecific noun.

   gender specific: The report referred to a *boy or girl* from the community.

gender neutral: The report referred to a *child* from the community.

3. Use an article, such as "the," rather than "his" or "her."

gender specific: During *his* interview, the reporter gave complicated answers.

gender neutral: During *the* interview, the reporter gave complicated answers.

4. Delete the pronoun.

gender specific: The director required *her* staff to arrive on time.

gender neutral: The director required staff to arrive on time.

Gender-Neutral Terminology

Table 4.1 presents a few examples of gender-specific terms and their gender-neutral equivalents.

TABLE 4.1   Gender-Specific and Gender-Neutral Language Forms

Gender Specific	Gender Neutral
policeman	police officer
waiter/waitress	food server
stewardess	flight attendant
mailman	postal worker
salesman	sales representative
TV anchorman	news anchor
mothering	parenting, nurturing
male nurse	nurse (specify gender only if important)
mankind	humanity
manmade	artificial or synthetic
manpower	workforce
housewife	home maker
man a project	staff a project
chairman or chairwoman	chair or chairperson
businessman or businesswoman	business executive or businessperson
congressman or congresswoman	congressional representative or member of Congress

Reducing Bias

APA (2020) provides guidelines for reducing bias by being specific (rather than general); some of those guidelines are summarized in Table 4.2.

TABLE 4.2   **APA Guidelines for Using Specificity to Reduce Bias**

Topic	General	Specific
age	broad categories of age, such as "over 65 years old"	Give exact age ranges, such as "65 to 75 years old."
disability	types of conditions, such as "a type of dementia"	Provide the name of the condition, such as "Alzheimer's disease."
gender identity	women or men	Use descriptors with modifiers, such as "cisgender women" and "transgender men."
research participants	people, children, or women	Indicate context, such as "patients," "participants," and "clients."
racial or ethnic groups	Latin Americans or Asian Americans	Include nation or region of origin, such as "Mexican Americans" or "Vietnamese Americans."
sexual orientation	broad group labels, such as "gay"	Use specific terms, such as "lesbians," "gay men," "bisexual people," or "straight people."
socioeconomic status	low income or high income	Give specific income ranges or designations, such as "below the poverty line."

Age-Appropriate Terms

While gerontologists use terms such as "young–old," "old–old," and "oldest–old," for APA style, define age groups by giving the specific age range for individuals in the study. Also, use the terms only as adjectives (or descriptors), such as "old–old individuals." In other words, do not use the descriptors as nouns; don't say "the old–old."

When referring to groups, use terms that are age appropriate:

- Use "men" and "women" instead of "males" and "females."
  - However, "males" and "females" are appropriate for groups that span a broad age range, such as a group that includes boys and men.
- For individuals under 12 years of age, appropriate terms include "child"; "girl"; "boy"; "transgender girl"; "transgender boy"; "gender-fluid child"; and, for the very young, "infant."
- For individuals aged 18 and older, use "adult," "woman," "man," "transgender man," "trans man," "transgender woman," and "cisgender adult," among others. (APA, 2020)

In general, avoid using generational descriptors. However, when discussing studies related to generational topics, it is appropriate to use generational descriptors such as "baby boomers," "Gen X," "Millennials," "Gen Z," and so on.

Gender Versus Sex

As you work with studies that address gender issues, use appropriate terminology. In recent years, the vocabulary for this area has been expanded and refined. To start, "gender identity" applies to all individuals and is distinct from sexual orientation.

Gender Identity Terminology

Use terms such as "identified pronouns," "self-identified pronouns," or "pronouns" rather than "preferred pronouns" (as "preferred" implies choice). Here are some terms related to gender:

- **binary:** when used in the context of gender, classifying gender in two distinct and opposite forms of masculine and feminine
- **cisgender:** a term used for individuals whose sex assigned at birth aligns with their gender identity
- **cisgenderism:** the belief that being cisgender is normative, as indicated by the assumption that individuals are cisgender unless otherwise specified
- **cissexism:** prejudice or discrimination against people who are transgender

- **gender:** a social construct that refers to the attitudes, feelings, and behaviors that a given culture associates with a person's biological sex; use the term "gender" when referring to people as social groups
- **genderism:** the belief that there are only two genders and that gender is automatically linked to an individual's sex assigned at birth
- **gender identity:** a person's psychological sense of their own gender
- **gender fluid:** a person who is nonbinary and whose gender varies from presumptions based on their sex assigned at birth
- **nonbinary gender:** a term that refers to a person who is gender fluid, genderqueer, gender nonconforming, gender neutral, agender, and so on
- **transgender:** a term used to refer to persons whose gender identity does not conform to what is culturally associated with their sex assigned at birth
- **transprejudice/transnegativity:** terms that denote discriminatory attitudes toward individuals who are transgender
- **TGNC:** an abbreviation for "transgender, nonconforming"

Scholars who conduct transgender, nonconforming (TGNC) psychological research use specific, descriptive language and avoid terms that are disparaging. Many individuals identifying as transgender, gender-nonconforming, or nonbinary also use specific, descriptive language.

Do *not* use: "birth sex," "natal sex," "tranny," or "transvestite"

Do use: "assigned sex" or "sex assigned at birth"

Do *not* use: "opposite gender" or "opposite sex"

Do use: "mixed gender," "mixed sex," "another sex," or "another gender"

- While the term "transsexual" is outdated, some people identify with it, and the word should be used for individuals who claim it.
- Use the term "gender" when referring to people as social groups.

Sexual Orientation

When writing about sexual orientation, use the following umbrella terms:

- sexual and gender minorities
- sexual orientation and gender diversity

The following are additional terms associated with sexual orientation:

- lesbian
- gay
- straight
- heterosexual
- bisexual
- asexual
- polysexual
- pansexual

Though the abbreviation "LGBT" is considered out of date; at this time, there is no consensus for which of the following abbreviations to use: LGBTQ, LGBTQ+, LGBTQIA, or LGBTQIA+. When you use a term that relates to sexual orientation or gender diversity, define it, and then specify the group you are writing about.

Race and Ethnicity

To avoid stereotyping of racial and ethnic groups, writers should be specific when using racial and ethnic terms. Here are terms for some racial and ethnic groups:

- African American (no hyphen) or Black (capitalized)
- Asian or Asian American (no hyphen)
- European American or White (capitalized)
- Indigenous or Indigenous People (when referring to a specific group, such as Indigenous People of North America)
- Native American (no hyphen)
- European Australian
- Aboriginal or Aboriginal People (when referring to a specific group, such as Aboriginal People of Australia or Indigenous Australians)
- Native Hawaiian or Pacific Islander

Once again, in your writing, use specific language (see Table 4.3).

TABLE 4.3   Specific Language Related to Race and Ethnicity

Nonspecific	Specific
Hispanic	Cuban Americans, Mexican Americans, Puerto Ricans, and so on
Latino, Latina	Mexicans, Brazilians, Nicaraguans, Cubans, Costa Ricans, and so on
Asian	Japanese, Chinese, Korean, Vietnamese, and so on
Middle Eastern, Arab	Egyptian, Iraqi, Jordanian, and so on

Be careful not to use terms such as "Hispanic," "Spanish," "Mexican," and "Latino/Latina" interchangeably, as they each have distinct meanings:

- **Spanish** is a language and also refers to people born in Spain.
- **Hispanic** is a broad term that refers to persons of Spanish-speaking origin or ancestry who share a connection to Spain.
- **Latino/Latina** refers to persons of Latin American heritage or origin who share a history of colonization from Spain.
- **Mexican** refers to Mexican citizens.
- **Chicano** refers to U.S. citizens of Mexican descent.

Also keep the following in mind when writing about race and ethnicity:

- Do not use "Afro-American," "negro," or "oriental."
- "People" should not be capitalized when referring to Indigenous or Aboriginal people *in general*, such as in "Indigenous people participated in the study."
- Do not hyphenate proper nouns, such as terms for race or ethnicity; for instance, "African American participants."
- When writing about specific races and ethnic groups, use the specific and preferred term for that group. Not all terms are listed here; do your research as necessary.

Disability: Unbiased Language and Labels

APA identifies two approaches to using disability language: *person-first language* and *identity-first language*. Consider the following when choosing an approach:

- **When you use person-first language,** you are emphasizing the person, not the person's disability or chronic condition (e.g., "people with substance use disorders" or "people with disabilities").
- **When you use identity-first language,** the disability becomes the focus (e.g., "substance abusers" or "the disabled").

Person-first language avoids putting labels on people. For example, when people are referred to as "the disabled," they are being objectified (or referred to as objects). In some contexts, however, identify-first language is often used as an expression of cultural pride and a reclamation of a disability that once conferred a negative identity (APA, 2020). Until you know what a person or group prefers, use person-first language (see Table 4.4).

TABLE 4.4   Identity-First and Person-First Language Forms

Identity-First Language	Person-First Language
schizophrenics	people who have schizophrenia
challenged	people who have challenges with …
wheelchair-bound	uses a wheelchair
AIDS victims	people with AIDS
high-risk groups	high-risk behavior
non-White	*the preference of the population*
minority	*the preference of the population*
Blacks	Black Americans, African Americans
senior citizen or oldster	a person who is 65 or elderly person
the elderly or the aged	elderly people
the disabled or the handicapped	people with disabilities
the lower class	people who are poor
the upper class	people with high incomes
the blind	people who are blind
the hearing impaired	people who are hard of hearing or deaf

Use Gender-Neutral and Unbiased Language

For all academic writing, be up to date with language usage, and put care into the language you use. Here are a few basic points:

1. Do not specify sex or gender, unless it is a variable or is essential to the discussion.
2. In general, do not label people; use person-first language, referring to people as *people*, not as *objects*. For example, use "people with disabilities," not "the disabled."
3. In specific cases, refer to people as they prefer to be called. For example, some people prefer identity-first language rather than person-first language. Though identify-first language is discouraged because it tends to objectify people, APA (2020) recommends the use of either, depending on an individual's preference.
4. Be specific about age, race, and culture.

To avoid gender reference, use plural nouns (when possible), and use "they" as a gender-neutral third-person pronoun. For more information, review Chapter 3.

Recap

As we've discussed, unbiased and gender-neutral writing and the associated terminology can be complicated. In addition, terminology that is unbiased and gender-neutral is new to many writers. For example, the 6th edition of the *Publication Manual of the American Psychological Association* (2009) did not cover these inclusive terms in such detail; and in a college curriculum, these terms would be covered primarily in advanced coursework that is specialized. Thus, when your writing focuses on content related to race, ethnicity, and gender as well as disability and aging, take the time to study the bias-free language guidelines that are discussed in the *Publication Manual for the American Psychological Association,* 7th edition (2020).

WRITING WORKSHOP

Gender-Neutral and Unbiased Language Exercise

Instructions: For the outdated and biased words and phrases below, provide a revised or alternate term. Also replace identity-first terms with person-first language.

Outdated	**Revised or Alternative**
1. congressman	_____
2. policeman	_____
3. waiter or waitress	_____
4. fireman	_____
5. mailman	_____
6. salesman	_____
7. TV anchorman	_____
8. mankind	_____
9. chairman	_____
10. bag lady	_____
11. male nurse	_____
12. Oriental	_____
13. Afro-American	_____
14. he/she or he or she	_____
15. boy or girl	_____
16. challenged	_____
17. wheelchair-bound	_____
18. AIDS victims	_____
19. high-risk groups	_____
20. nonwhite	_____
21. minority	_____
22. the disabled or the handicapped	_____

23. the lower class _____

24. the blind _____

25. the old–old _____

ACTIVITY KEY

Gender-Neutral and Unbiased Language Exercise

Outdated	Revised or Alternative
1. congressman	congressional representative
2. policeman	police officer
3. waiter or waitress	wait staff or server
4. fireman	fire fighter
5. mailman	mail carrier
6. salesman	salesperson
7. TV anchorman	TV anchor
8. mankind	humankind
9. chairman	chair or chairperson
10. bag lady	homeless person
11. male nurse	nurse
12. Oriental	Asian
13. Afro-American	African American
14. he/she or he or she	they
15. boy or girl	child
16. challenged	people who have challenges
17. wheelchair-bound	uses a wheelchair
18. AIDS victims	people with AIDS
19. high-risk groups	high-risk behavior
20. non-White	*the preference of the population*
21. minority	*the preference of the population*
22. the disabled or the handicapped	people with disabilities

23. the lower class	people who are poor
24. the blind	people who are blind
25. the old–old	old–old individuals

References

American Sociological Association. (2014). *American Sociological Association style guide* (5th ed.).

American Psychological Association. (2009). *Publication manual for the American Psychological Association* (6th ed.). https://doi.org/10.1037/0000165-000

American Psychological Association. (2020). *Publication manual for the American Psychological Association* (7th ed.). https://doi.org/10.1037/0000165-000

National Association of Social Workers. (February 11, 2021). *NASW press guidelines for describing people*. https://naswpress.org/content/1430

National Center on Disability and Journalism. (August 2021). *Disability language style guide*. Retrieved February 8, 2022, from http://ncdj.org/style-guide/

PART II

Writing Your Paper

5

INTRODUCTION, THESIS, AND CONCLUSION

Writing is a process, and some parts of that process are more difficult than others. For example, getting started may be the most difficult part, which is one reason you shouldn't necessarily attempt to write the introduction first.

In fact, "getting started" isn't even about sitting down to write your paper; after you select your topic, the next steps are to research, read, and reflect, until you gain understanding that leads to insight. Though it is important to write while you are "cooking your ideas," don't expect results—getting fleeting insights on the page is a small but important step.

When you do start writing for results, write about what you know first. In other words, start writing the body, summarizing key points, and fleshing out themes. In fact, you might even write your conclusion before you write your introduction; the two are linked.

If you have a choice on topics, select one that interests you most; motivation to learn about your topic creates momentum for your writing. And if you develop a passion for learning about your topic, your writing may take on "a life of its own." Do you know that feeling? When you make that kind of connection with your writing, your insights can lead to peak learning experiences, making the entire process feel almost magical.

When you complete this chapter, you will be able to

- develop a strategy for identifying a topic or problem,
- identify why your problem matters,
- write a purpose statement and thesis,
- apply the CARS model to writing introductory paragraphs for research writing,
- use the PEER model for planning and organizing, and
- write an introduction that links to the conclusion.

While APA style focuses on citations, formatting, and much more, APA does not specifically address how to organize or structure your paper beyond recommending that your paper be "clear, precise, and logical" (2020). Therefore, this chapter provides guidelines for producing evidence-based scholarly writing organized in a traditional structure. While this chapter reviews information about working with your topic, Chapter 6 goes into greater depth about selecting credible sources for your research.

The Introduction

Academic writing is evidence based and strives for clarity; it also follows a traditional format by

- offering a central idea through a clear introduction
- developing the idea through well-supported body paragraphs
- providing resolution in a conclusion

In the introduction, state your purpose and give an overview of your paper. Though the thesis statement can be presented anywhere in the introduction, generally it comes toward the end of the first paragraph so that it is placed in context. In addition, to awaken your reader's curiosity, you may wish to pose questions about your topic or use a quotation to draw interest.

The aforementioned "formula" might sound easy, until you actually start writing your introduction. A graduate student once related that they spent six months thinking about how to start their master's paper. So in frustration, they started in the middle, which led to conclusions.

Only in retrospect did the student understand that writing an introduction first was not even a possibility.

The most painful part of writing might be the learning curve that comes with a new topic. Thus, until you have a clear sense of purpose, writing an effective introduction is not feasible. To avoid "spinning your wheels," do your groundwork, until you know your topic well.

Write about what you know; once you start putting your thoughts on paper, one idea will lead to the next. Then continue to trust the process. Do the work and embrace the challenges, knowing that each tiny step propels you forward. In other words, action dissolves fear. Become immersed in each step; the more you read and think about your topic, the more your ideas will flow.

What Is Your Topic?

Do you have a strong interest in a current issue in your field? If you are unsure of your interests, talk to peers, visit topically oriented research sites, review course readings, and browse current journals. Consider the following when selecting your topic:

- **Select a topic that is manageable.** A topic that is too broad can be overwhelming, and a topic that is too narrow may not provide sufficient resources.
- **Make a list of concepts and terms.** Use those keywords to search your library's databases. (On other online sites, you may find articles that are not peer reviewed; you may also find advocacy sites that charge a fee or present unvalidated research.)

If at any time you need guidance, speak to your librarian. Librarians are versed in all fields, and helping you is part of their purpose for being there.

What Is the Problem?

Rather than focus on finding a topic, determine whether there a question in your field that intrigues you or an issue that fascinates you. For example, academic writing involves arguing problems; it also involves "unraveling puzzles." Think of your topic as a problem to explore. As you probe issues you also extend your knowledge.

Identifying the problem brings you closer to developing your thesis question. When you find your problem, you will find your question. In addition, the problem will help validate the "why," answering the question "So what?" (APA, 2020). These are questions that you will develop in your introduction and your purpose statement, if you write one.

What Is Your Question?

Define your topic or problem as a question, developing a clear, focused, and complex research question (Indiana University, n.d.):

- **clear:** Include enough detail so that your question expresses the concrete elements of your inquiry.

  unclear: Do health care workers have an impact on infectious disease?

  clear: What are specific practices of health care workers that affect infectious disease rates?

- **focus**: Narrow your focus so that it is specific rather than too broad to be explored in a meaningful way.

  unfocused: What role does good hygiene play for health care workers?

  focused: When health care workers clean their hands before and after each patient visit, what are the benefits?

- **complexity**: Develop a question that needs analysis rather than a "simple" answer.

  too simple: Why do some parents neglect their children?

  complex: What are the biopsychosocial causes of child neglect?

Your question is the basis for your thesis statement. Read more about your topic, and discuss it with your peers, professor, and librarian.

As previously mentioned, writing is a process. Before trying to write your thesis statement, explore the research until you gain enough insight to identify a problem or "puzzle" that intrigues you.

Why Is Your Question Important?

Academic writing can help you explore "burning issues," and your writing may even serve a broader purpose by filling a knowledge gap in the field. Consider the following when determining the importance of your question:

1. What is the purpose? Why is it relevant?
2. What value does your question have? What benefits will result?
3. Is your topic controversial? Are there debates about it? What are the various viewpoints?
4. Is your topic important at the local, national, or international level?
5. Is your topic a current issue? Does it have historical relevance?
6. Why does it matter? Does it pass the "So what?" test?
7. Does it relate to arguing a point or analyzing an issue?

Finding the Right Resources

In this era of misinformation, using scholarly and peer-reviewed studies is critical.

Selecting books that inform your topic can provide depth and breadth not found in journal articles. For example, *edited texts* often have multiple authors addressing the same topic.

Look at publication dates; unless you are seeking historical perspectives, select resources that are within the last 10 years. Review the background of authors; for scholarly work, do not select books by celebrities. *When was the text published? Has it been revised over time?*

FIGURE 5.1 **Using Scholarly Research**

Purpose Statements and Theses

Purpose is at the core of all writing, and most academic writing defines purpose through a *thesis statement.* A thesis statement presents the topic, problem, or argument and lets the reader know how the topic will be developed. An additional way to enhance your planning process is by writing a *purpose statement.* A purpose statement provides information about why you chose your topic, summarizing your aim or focus.

Purpose Statements

Purpose is the principal element of all writing. If your professor needs to approve your topic, write a purpose statement in which you discuss why you selected your topic and why it is important. You can then use key points in your purpose statement to introduce your thesis.

Writing a brief purpose statement also helps you clarify your thinking and enhances the planning process, answering the "So what?" question. Here are some questions to get you started:

- What is your question?
- What value does it have?
- Why does it matter?

For an academic paper, introduce the thesis statement with a purpose statement:

> **first draft:** The purpose of this paper is to examine whether training nurses outside of the labor and delivery department can improve the outcomes of providing a safe environment for the mother and newborn when delivery occurs in the emergency room.

As you revise your statement, avoid using the word "purpose":

> **revised:** Many babies are born in unexpected places, including the emergency room. In these situations, expectant mothers experience added stress. This paper examines the kinds of training for emergency room nurses that can alleviate some of the stress, improving the outcomes for unplanned deliveries that occur there.

A purpose statement should lead to your thesis statement, giving readers an overview of the problem and its importance. Present your thesis statement toward the end of the first paragraph.

Thesis Statements

A thesis statement expresses a unique and specific point about your topic, unifying the content of the entire paper. An effective thesis statement is specific and makes a strong assertion that can be supported with evidence (Lumen Learning, n.d.). In other words, you are not simply stating your topic; you are making a claim about it and arguing your position in a clear and confident style.

Start by identifying whether you are developing an argument or analyzing a topic or issue:

- For an argument, identify an issue that can be argued.
  - What is your argument? What is your claim?
  - What is your evidence?
  - Why is it significant?
- For an analysis, identify a complex topic or process.
  - What are the component parts of the topic?
  - What are the relationships among those parts?
  - What is your claim? What evidence supports it?
  - Does it matter? If so, why?

Start the process by defining your problem—your core question. For example, let us say your thesis relates to arguing whether providing additional training to nurses in an emergency room improves outcomes for childbirth. Start by stating the problem as a question.

> **thesis question:** Few events cause more stress for emergency room staff than an unexpected birth. Would additional nurse training in childbirth improve outcomes for unplanned deliveries in the emergency room?

Next, turn your question into a statement.

> **rephrased as a statement:** Additional training for nurses improves outcomes for unplanned deliveries that occur in the emergency room.

Finally, once you understand some of the broader implications of your question, draft a thesis statement that reflects your argument.

> **thesis statement:** When emergency room nurses receive training in childbirth, outcomes improve for both mother and child when an unplanned delivery occurs in the emergency room.

Let us turn one more problem into a thesis statement. For example, here is how you could work through a topic addressing emotional support for chemotherapy patients.

> **thesis question:** Cancer patients experience extreme uncertainty about a multitude of issues while they are undergoing treatment. What resources are available to provide emotional support for patients undergoing chemotherapy? What impact does it have?

Next, turn your question into a thesis statement.

> **thesis statement**: When chemotherapy patients receive emotional support, their outlook changes significantly, having a positive effect on diagnosis.

Once again, an effective thesis statement is specific and makes a strong assertion that can be supported with evidence. Can you identify the claim and how evidence can be used to argue the position presented in the previous example? When you write about a topic/ problem that intrinsically interests you, your motivation will assist you in writing a strong assertion and argument en route to solving the problem.

Remember that writing is not a linear process. At times, you will discover data that has an impact on your thesis statement; modify your thesis based on new information, as needed. The introduction presents your thesis, body paragraphs provide evidence to support your thesis, and the conclusion summarizes the results, tying back to the introduction and the thesis statement.

Introduction: Article Summary

The type of introduction you write depends largely on the type of assignment you are writing. For example, when you are summarizing an article, give a complete reference in the introduction. Include the author's last name, the name of the article or book, and its purpose.

> In the article entitled "Internet Addiction and Excessive Social Network Use: What About Facebook?" Guedes et al. (2018) explored the use and overuse of Facebook and even addiction to Facebook.

Throughout the summary, refer to authors and other subjects by last name only. In fact, for all academic writing in APA style, refer to authors only by their last name.

Introduction for Research Papers: The CARS Model

For scholarly research papers, common patterns have been identified for introducing topics. One pattern identified by John Swales is known as the *creating a research space (CARS) model*. The CARS model reveals three rhetorical moves made in most research introductions (Swales & Feak, 2008). As you review the following questions take note of their relevance for writing in the health sciences and other fields.

Move 1: Establishing a Research Territory

What is the significance of your research?

1. Show that the research area is important, central, interesting, problematic, or relevant.
2. Introduce and review items of previous research.

Move 2: Establishing a Niche

What are the limitations of previous studies?

1. Identify gaps in previous research.
2. Raise questions.
3. Indicate how you will extend knowledge.

Move 3: Occupying the Niche

How does your work contribute? How is your paper organized?

1. Outline purposes, or state the nature of the present research.
2. List research questions or hypotheses.
3. Announce principal findings.
4. State the value of the present research.
5. Indicate the structure of the research paper.

Writing an Introduction

When using the CARS model, writing your introduction last can be an effective approach. For example, most of the questions posed in the model could not be answered prior to much research and reflection. As you write about your topic, you gain insight and depth; key points take on significance. For topics that have meaning for you, your research fuels your passion for resolving your thesis.

Figure 5.2 shows the introductory paragraph of a paper entitled *Treatments for Depression in Elderly Patients*. The paper was written by Tolson (2019), an MSW student at Indiana University Northwest. Can you identify the thesis statement? What evidence supports the value of the question and why this problem matters?

The PEER Model

The *purpose, evidence, explanation, resolve (PEER) model* helps you focus on the purpose of each part of your essay or paper. Use the PEER model to ensure you have developed all relevant aspects:

- **P:** What is the purpose?
  - What are the key points, and why are they relevant?
- **E:** What evidence demonstrates the main points?
  - What are the facts and details?
- **E:** What do readers need to understand the evidence and its significance?
  - What explanation or examples support the evidence?
- **R:** How can you resolve your thesis for your readers?
  - What key points provide a recap?
  - What are your conclusions and recommendations?

Treatments for Depression in Elderly Patients

The elderly is a population that is at an increased risk of developing a depressive disorder. Although many consider depression to be a normal part of aging, it is recognized as a chronic medical condition. According to the CDC, "An estimated 13 percent of the elderly population is diagnosed with major depressive disorder and an even higher percentage being diagnosed with mild depressive disorder" (CDC, 2017). Many older adults go untreated because symptoms are mistaken as life changes, medical illnesses, or patients themselves fail to seek care. However, depression in the elderly can be treated. Currently, there are many options to treat depression in older adults including cognitive behavioral therapy, medication, physical activity, art therapy, and music therapy. Because treatment options work for different patients, what would be the most effective treatment for this population?

FIGURE 5.2   Writing an Introduction

When composing, create a template, using side headings to rough out your ideas. If you loosely apply the peer model as you compose, your content will be somewhat structured before you revise.

When revising, evaluate whether you have developed your topic adequately with specific evidence and examples. Would your evidence convince a person who was undecided about the topic?

The Conclusion

Just as your introduction provides an overview of what is to come, your conclusion provides a summary of results. You are giving a general overview of the findings and whether they support your thesis. When you write your conclusion, your aim is to bring resolution for your reader. In other words, you are placing findings in context, bringing the reader to a sense of closure, while also opening the reader to the logical next steps:

- Link major arguments to your research question or thesis.
- Summarize key findings, conveying the importance of your work.
- Answer questions that you posed in the introduction.
- Identify gaps; what should be explored next?
- Share your own reflections; what did you learn from your research?
- Do not include new information in your conclusion.

Figure 5.3 shows the conclusion to the paper on treating elderly patients for depression shown in Figure 5.2 (Tolson, 2019). How does the conclusion tie back to the introduction? Does the conclusion resolve the question posed in the introduction?

Conclusion

As with hypertension and diabetes, depression is a treatable

medical condition and not just a normal part of aging (CDC, 2017).

It is a common problem that can interfere with an elderly person's

ability to function. Depression is different for older adults because

they are at an increased risk and are often misdiagnosed. Although

many treatments reduce the symptoms of depression including

FIGURE 5.3   Writing a Conclusion

physical exercise, medication, art therapy, and music therapy, CBT has been proven to be the most effective treatment. Research has shown that CBT is cost effective and has long-term benefits with no side effects or risk of interaction with other medications.

Even though CBT has been well documented as a valuable treatment, further studies need to be performed on music and art therapy. Additionally, most people are living longer because of new findings in healthcare research, so the old-old population (over age 85) must be an area of focus when discussing depression treatments.

FIGURE 5.3 **Writing a Conclusion (*Continued*)**

Recap

Include a thesis statement in the first paragraph of the work, restating it with depth and resolution in the conclusion. As your project progresses, revisit your thesis statement, refining it as needed. As you write your introduction and the body of your paper, consider using the CARS or PEER model. These models can assist you in staying organized, ensuring you cover important elements of your paper.

WRITING WORKSHOP

Part 1: Analyzing Purpose

Instructions: Select a paper you have written or the draft of a current assignment. If possible, exchange your paper with a peer. Analyze the assignment by answering the questions below. Then give each other feedback and take notes so that you can apply the feedback to a possible revision.

1. Thesis Statement

    1.1   Can you identify the thesis of the paper? What is it?

    1.2   Does a purpose statement effectively introduce the thesis?

    1.3   Is the paper an argument or an analysis?

    1.4   Does the author answer the "So what?" question?

2. Introduction, Body, and Conclusion

    2.1   Does the introduction give an overview of the paper?

    2.2   Is information presented logically, or are there gaps?

    2.3   Is the conclusion tied to the thesis or questions posed in the introduction?

    2.4   Does the paper effectively resolve the question it poses? Please explain.

    2.5   Do you have suggestions for changes or additions to the content?

3. Viewpoint

    3.1   What pronoun viewpoint(s) did the writer use throughout the paper?

    3.2   Are authors who are cited in the paper referred to by last name?

    3.3   Does the writer need to make changes to voice or viewpoint? If so, how?

Part 2: Process Message

Instructions: Write your professor a process message.

1. If you have a current assignment, write your professor a purpose statement explaining your project, your progress, and your next steps.

2. If you completed the exercise in Part 1, what are some things you learned?

TIME MANAGEMENT

To gain maximum value of your time, acknowledge your anxiety, and embrace the process. Make a plan based on *backtiming*. Backtiming refers to setting internal deadlines starting from the due date and working backwards.

Deadlines have a psychological impact, so use them to your advantage. Then do not expect the first draft of any part of your paper to be perfect; that's the purpose of editing.

Academic Papers

Introduction

In your introduction, state your purpose, connecting its relevance to your audience.

- Give an overview of the topic and state your thesis.
- Pose questions about your topic: *what am I writing about and why?*
  What is my general purpose ... my specific purpose?
  What are my main points?
  Who are my readers and how can I shape my writing for them?

Body

In the body of your paper, provide evidence. Focus on key points and give concrete examples; avoid generalizations not substantiated by data.

- Break your topic into component parts; use side headings.
- When applicable, break your paper into sections, such as *methods*, *results*, and *discussion*.
- Support all main points with evidence (data) and cite the sources.

FIGURE 5.4   **Basic Structure for Academic Papers**

Conclusion

In your conclusion, provide resolution for the problem. Answer questions that you may have posed in the introduction, drawing conclusions for your reader. Finally, make sure conclusions are based on data; identify gaps in the research and glance forward to next steps, if relevant.

When you write your conclusion, revisit your introduction and align your thesis statement to the outcomes in your conclusion.

FIGURE 5.4   **Basic Structure for Academic Papers (*Continued*)**

References

American Psychological Association. (2020). *Publication manual of the American Psychological Association* (7th ed.). https://doi.org/10.1037/0000165-000

Indiana University. (n.d.). *Develop a research question.* https://libraries.indiana.edu/sites/default/files/Develop_a_Research_Question.pdf

Lumen Learning. (n.d.). *Developing a Strong, Clear Thesis Statement.* Retrieved August 3, 2022, from https://courses.lumenlearning.com/suny-ccc-engl-1010-1/chapter/developing-a-strong-clear-thesis-statement/

Swales, J. M., & Feak, C. B. (2008). *Academic writing for graduate students.* University of Michigan Press.

Tolson, T. (2019). *Treatments for depression in elderly patients.* Indiana University Northwest, Social Work Department.

University of Southern California. Organizing your social science research paper: The research problem/question. https://libguides.usc.edu/writingguide/introduction/researchproblem

6

ANNOTATED BIBLIOGRAPHIES, ABSTRACTS, AND GRAPHICS

A s you write abstracts and prepare annotated bibliographies, you hone your skills at identifying credible sources and analyzing articles. More importantly, you are developing a foundation for your future area of expertise.

As Dewey once said,

> We sometimes talk as if "original research" were a peculiar pre-rogative of scientists or at least of advanced students. But all thinking is research, and all research is native, original, with him who carries it on, even if everybody else in the world already is sure of what he is still looking for. (1967, p. 148)

In other words, you do not need to be the author of a study to achieve enlightening results; each time you have a significant insight, you are experiencing "original research." Thus, as you chase down sources, gaining insight and knowledge, you may have peak learning experiences, especially if you have a passion for what you are learning. Synthesizing data is a form of research that has its own rewards.

Credible research enhances humankind by illuminating truth. But even research done well can be twisted and distorted, setting back efforts rather than catapulting a field forward. One of your goals now is to review how to select articles that come from credible sources. To assist you in presenting your research, this chapter also covers constructing basic graphics.

When you complete this chapter, you will be able to

- create and format an annotated bibliography,
- select scholarly resources using credible sources,
- write an abstract,
- review basics for using charts, graphs, and tables, and
- incorporate graphics into an APA paper.

Annotated Bibliography

At times, an annotated bibliography is a complete project of its own; at other times, professors require annotated bibliographies to be written in preparation for a larger assignment, such as a literature review. As you select scholarly articles, books, and other resources, begin your annotated bibliography by writing a paragraph that describes and evaluates each resource of value, assessing its relevance and quality. In fact, you can think of an annotated bibliography as a collection of notes to yourself; if you do write a literature review, this approach helps you organize materials.

Since there are different types of annotated bibliographies, check with your instructor so that you can shape it to your instructor's requirements for content, structure, and length:

- A *descriptive* or *informative* annotated bibliography includes a paragraph that describes the source and summarizes the content.
- An *analytical* or a *critical* annotated bibliography goes beyond summarizing content by analyzing each source for purpose, relevance, and quality:
  - Who are the authors and what are their credentials?
  - What type of article is it and for what type of audience?
  - What is its purpose or relevance to your topic?

○ What are the strengths, weaknesses, and possible biases?
○ Is the article useful for your project? (Cornell University, 2022)

As you review each source, you are starting the comparative analysis of your literature review. Here is the citation information to collect:

- author(s)
- title of article, journal title, date of publication, volume number, and issue number
- title of book, publisher, year of publication, and page numbers
- digital object identifier (DOI), if applicable

Format each resource by placing your brief summary or analysis of the content below the basic citation information:

- For the citation, use hanging indentation style; block the first line at the left margin, and indent subsequent lines 0.5 inches.
- For your annotation, which may consist of multiple paragraphs, indent the first line of each paragraph 0.5 inches.
- Aim for each annotated bibliography to be between 100 and 200 words in length, or longer, depending on your purpose.

One way to organize an annotation is using these three categories: summary, assessment, and reflection. Use these categories as subheadings for each source you annotate (see Figure 6.1).

Figure 6.1 shows an example of an annotated bibliography written by Tolson (2019), an MSW student at Indiana University Northwest. Tolson wrote eight annotated bibliographies before synthesizing the information in a literature review entitled *Treatments for Depression in Elderly Patients*.

Abstract

An abstract is a short summary, no longer than 250 words, that gives an overview of the content of a paper and includes the following:

- What is the problem?
  ○ What are your questions or arguments?
  ○ What is your thesis or hypothesis?

Annotated Bibliography, Article 3

Alduhishy, M. (2018). The overprescription of antidepressants and

its impact on the elderly in Australia. *Trends in Psychiatry and*

Psychotherapy, 40(3), 241-243.

Summary of Article. In terms of effectiveness, anti-depressants

have changed very little over the years, but overprescribing and

adverse side effects are still prevalent. Alduhishy (2018) found that

the use of antidepressants in the elderly have increased substantially.

Use of antidepressants causes an economic problem for this popula-

tion, and patients tend to search for an alternative type of treatment.

The elderly population who have been prescribed selective serotonin

reuptake inhibitors (SSRIs) have an increased risk of falling, which

raises their chances of developing other serious medical conditions.

This article also found that for every year the patient remains on the

medication, their mortality rate increases.

Assessment. Alduhishy is a resident medical officer at the

Rockhampton Hospital in Australia. This article was published in

the journal of *Trends in Psychiatry and Psychotherapy* in 2018.

Reflection. While working in healthcare, I have always felt

that anti-depressants are overly prescribed to elderly patients.

FIGURE 6.1   Annotated Bibliography

Studies show that (SSRIs) such as Paxil and Lexapro demonstrate insignificant results in elderly patients diagnosed with mild or moderate depression. According to Alduhishy (2018), "Psychotherapy, e.g., cognitive behavioral therapy (CBT), supportive clinical care including psychoeducation and teaching the patient problem solving skills are the first line of therapy." If psychotherapy and similar non-pharmaceutical treatments are the first line of therapy, then why are physicians so eager to prescribe medication? Could it be because of the physician-pharmaceutical company relationship? When research is done by pharmaceutical companies, is bias involved? Comparable articles also support the use of non-pharmaceutical interventions in the treatment of depression.

FIGURE 6.1 **Annotated Bibliography** (*Continued*)

- If applicable, what are your methods?
- What are your findings, results, and conclusions?
- Why does it matter?
  - What is the significance?
  - What are the implications? (Streefkerk, 2020)

An abstract informs readers whether a paper is relevant for their research; as such, it must be an accurate reflection of the content of the paper. Do not include information in the abstract that does not appear in the paper. APA (2020a, p. 13) also stresses that the abstract should "report rather than evaluate" the content; do not include your own interpretations or comments.

While an abstract is required for papers submitted for publication, for student papers, include an abstract when your instructor requires it. If your instructor requires a structured abstract, include the following sections: objective, method, results, and conclusions. Set these section headings in bold, italic font (APA, 2020, p. 13).

In addition, if you are submitting a paper for publication, APA guidelines may not be sufficient. Check with the journal to identify their unique submission guidelines, which may differ from APA requirements. Be sure to tailor your abstract to the expectations of your field. In addition, the *Publication Manual of the American Psychological Association* (2020) provides guidelines for what to include in the abstract for different kinds of papers, such as empirical studies, literature review or meta-analyses, theoretical papers, methodological papers, and case studies.

Use the following guidelines when creating an abstract:

- Place the abstract on page 2 (immediately after the title page).
- Use the title "Abstract," formatted as a level-1 heading (centered and in bold).
- Start the body of the abstract a double space below the heading (don't add extra space).
- Do not indent the first line of the abstract.
- Include a keyword summary a double space below the body of the abstract (once again, do not add extra space).
- Indent the keyword summary 0.5 inches, and italicize "Keywords." (Writing Center, University of Wisconsin-Madison, n.d.)

For the keyword summary, select three to five words and phrases from the abstract that effectively reflect the content of your paper (e.g., *Keywords:* word 1, word 2, word 3, and so on). Select keywords that will aid readers in locating your paper through an online search.

Do not capitalize the keywords, unless they are proper nouns. Separate the words with a comma, and do not place a period at the end. Figure 6.2 shows the abstract written by Tolson (2019), an MSW student at Indiana University Northwest, for Tolson's literature review, entitled *Treatments for Depression in Elderly Patients*.

Abstract

Depression is the most common mental health illness affecting the elderly. This literature review will examine eight articles that have researched the treatments for depression. The aim of this review is to explore current treatment options for the elderly to determine which is most effective in reducing the symptoms of depression. Symptoms of depression include fatigue, irritability, withdrawal, sleep problems, and changes in appetite. Treatments such as cognitive behavioral therapy, physical exercise, art therapy, music therapy, and anti-depressant medication are all remedies used to treat mild to major depression in the elderly population. The research methods include single-blind and double-blind controlled studies to compare patients ages 65 and over to control groups. Each article examines the advantages and risks to determine which treatment is the most beneficial. Short-term and long-term effects were also examined as part of the research. Although physical exercise and medication were effective in treating depression, cognitive behavioral therapy was equally as effective and had fewer risk factors associated compared with other treatments.

FIGURE 6.2 Abstract

Keywords: depression, elderly, cognitive behavioral therapy, anti-depressant medication, treatment, physical activity, art and music therapy

FIGURE 6.2   Abstract *(Continued)*

Journal Article Review

As you review articles and books, you are applying critical reading and thinking skills. Reading critically involves critiquing the structure of an article as well as analyzing its content.

When you read one article critically, you engage in an active process that involves questioning and interpreting. When you synthesize information from multiple articles, you apply critical thinking skills to categorize and group information, compare and contrast methods and results, and identify gaps and omissions in the literature.

What Makes a Journal Article Scholarly?

Articles published in academic journals are considered *scholarly* because they are written by experts in the field for other experts, such as faculty, researchers, practitioners, subject specialists, and other scholars. In addition, they have generally been *juried*, which means that they have been peer-reviewed or refereed prior to being approved for publication.

The *peer-review process* consists of sending the article to other researchers to analyze and assess its academic merit to the field. When an article does not meet standards, the author is given feedback and may be given the option to revise the article and resubmit it. However, academic journals generally put a limit on the number of times an article can be resubmitted.

At times, articles are not accepted because the writing is unclear, even though the research has merit. Effective editing skills make a difference, especially as it relates to publishing research.

A *refereed article* is sent out for peer review *blind*, meaning the reviewers do not know the name of the author, and the author is not told the names of the reviewers. This anonymity ensures that a work is judged on its merit rather than the author's reputation.

To find scholarly journal articles in your field, use your library databases. For example, for health care, use PubMed Central (PMC).

While articles published in popular magazines or found on websites may be informative and interesting, they lack the credibility of juried articles. Articles in popular magazines are often written with a slant to promote an idea, product, person, or theory.

One critical standard of scholarly articles is that they present findings in an unbiased way. However, even articles published in scholarly journals need to be evaluated with an open mind. For example, the following questions need to be considered: Is credible research being excluded? Are contrary views being discounted without trustworthy evidence?

What Is Your Selection Strategy?

When you start to examine articles, develop a plan to identify the most relevant articles efficiently. By reading the abstract, introduction, and conclusion first, you learn if the article applies to your question. If it seems relevant, then know when to *skim*, when to *scan*, and when to *read* an article thoroughly:

- **Scan** an article to find whether it contains relevant information. When you scan, focus on keywords and key phrases; when you find a keyword, read the text before and after it carefully.
- **Skim** an article to get a quick overview. When you skim, read rapidly through key parts to evaluate whether an article has worth for your purpose; key parts include the abstract, headings, introductory paragraph, topic sentences, and summaries.
- **Read** an article thoroughly when you are including it in your analysis. Apply your critical reading skills to seek a deep understanding of the thesis the authors are developing. Read it more than once, and take notes or highlight sections that are relevant.

Once you have selected several well-written juried journal articles, review them individually. As part of the process, you may need to create an annotated bibliography for your comparative analysis or critique of the literature.

ARTICLE REVIEW

Examine a journal article in your field. Read the introduction and the conclusion; identify the thesis statement, and consider how the article is summarized:

- How do the authors structure their literature review?
- In the literature review section, how are the various authors introduced?
- What evidence is provided, and how do the authors present it?
- How is the data presented and analyzed?
- How relevant is it to your topic?

Journal Article Review: The Process

Let's take a look at a step-by-step process for completing a journal article review. Read through all six steps, focusing on the kinds of questions to reflect upon while reviewing each article.

Step 1: Select an Article[1]

While you want to keep your search up to date, you do not want to overlook older studies that contain substance and relevance. Before you read an article or chapter, ask yourself the following:

- What is the title, and who are the authors? What are their credentials?
- What is the research problem, central question, or hypothesis?
- Does the article contain original research?
- How is the article organized? What are the headings and subheadings?
- Where does this article fit into your understanding of the field?

---

1   Your professor may allow you to use a chapter from a book, giving you the guidelines and criteria for your selection.

Read the abstract, introduction, and conclusion of the article to see if it informs your thesis or other themes and topics in your literature review. Next, look at the references. Who do the authors reference? Do they reference their own work? Do they cite articles from mainstream academic journals? While checking out their references, see if any of those articles relate to your question. If an article is a good fit for your research, you may want to review the original article.

Step 2: Summarize the Article

- What are the basic details of the purpose, methods, and conclusion?
  - What did the authors do?
  - How did they do it? (methodology)
  - Why did they do it?
  - What were the outcomes of the study?
- How is it relevant to your topic?
- Who is the article about and not about? (For example, consider age, ethnicity, gender, and location.)

Step 3: Analyze the Literature Review

A critical part of research articles is a review of the literature, which provides the context for the thesis or the hypothesis. As you read the review of the literature, ask yourself the following:

- What are the themes? Did the authors use headings to identify each theme?
- How did the authors integrate the literature within each theme?
- What are the points of agreement and points of conflict or disagreement?

Step 4: Analyze the Research

As you analyze the content of an article, also pay attention to the structure and flow of the article. Good examples provide excellent models for your writing. As you read each article, ask yourself the following:

- Is the research quantitative, qualitative, or both?

- For quantitative research articles, what are the independent and dependent variables?
- Is the research exploratory, explanatory, or descriptive?
- What are the sources for the data? What methods are used to collect and analyze the data?
- What are the theoretical assumptions?
- What is the context for the experimental design?
  - Are the authors comparing the effects of sugar-laden cereal with candy or unsweetened oatmeal?
  - Are the authors comparing a new drug with a drug that has already been shown to have serious side effects and detrimental outcomes?
  - Are the authors comparing health benefits of bacon with lunch meat or comparing bacon with beans and vegetables?
- What are the operational definitions?
  - How are the definitions similar to or different from those used by others?
- Were the samples an accurate representation? Who was not included in the study?
- What conclusions do the authors reach?

Analyzing research with an open mind is critical. When profit motives are involved, results must be evaluated in a broad context that

OPERATIONAL DEFINITIONS: GROUP LABELS

Research involves concepts and abstractions, which must be made concrete so that observation and measurement are possible. An *operational definition* is the way a researcher measures a variable.

When you define a group, describe participants clearly, and make sure to avoid terms that could sound biased or pejorative. For example, rather than saying "drug users," define the group as "Group A, people who use drugs." In general, use person-first language (e.g., "people with disabilities") rather than identify-first language (e.g., "the disabled").

puts outcomes in perspective. For example, for decades now, industries have been known to distort research and then publicize "slogans" and mistruths to mislead consumers. Can you think of any prominent examples?

Step 5: Define the Outcomes

While all studies have limitations and biases, good studies discuss their limitations and possible sources of bias. As you read the article, ask yourself the following:

- What results were reported? What evidence supports their conclusions?
- Did the article answer the questions it set out to explore? If not, why?
- Could intervening variables (e.g., people, things, or events) have interfered with the research, leading to inaccurate results?
- What are the strengths and weaknesses of the methodology? Did the authors of the research study identify strengths and weaknesses of the research as well as gaps?
- Did personal ideology influence the methodology or outcomes?
- Who paid for or benefited from the research?
- What are the affiliations of the researchers?
  - Did the authors list conflicts of interest?
  - Have you done a further check of the authors' affiliations and sponsors?
- Did the authors identify areas for further research?
- Finally, what could the authors have done differently?

WHAT ARE THE PATTERNS, THEMES, OR COMMON THREADS?

Common threads are considered objective data and can more readily be generalized. As you review various theories, look for common themes or characteristics. Ask yourself the following: What information does everyone seem to hold in common?

Now more than ever, research needs to be evaluated with skepticism. For example, even established journals have published misinformation that has needed to be retracted. As a researcher, when you feel uncomfortable about outcomes or when results seem "too good to be true," trust your gut, and do additional digging and probing.

Step 6: Recap or Reflection

For each article, write a brief summary of your findings that you can use for your annotated bibliography as well as a critique of the literature. As you review each article, take special note of common themes and patterns, as these will be a focus of your comparative analysis or synthesis.

- Does the information contribute to your thesis? If so, how?
- How does the information in the article compare or contrast with information in other scholarly articles or books?
- Did the authors integrate or synthesize the various articles into themes?
- Based on unanswered questions or gaps, is there a need for more research?
- How does the literature reviewed in the article connect to your thesis? Are original articles cited that merit reading?

Research

When working with research, an important quality is keeping an open mind to innovative and diverse ideas—thinking "outside of the box," so to speak.

Exploring possibilities involves suspending judgment. Your mind is open when you evaluate evidence and consider possibilities; an open mind contributes to adapting to change and giving people a chance to prove themselves before drawing a conclusion. For example, it is easy to become overly attached to what you assume you know. Here are two examples:

- At one time, it was believed that the world was flat. Galileo was brought to trial, publicly humiliated, and condemned of heresy because he challenged that belief.

- In 1982 two Australian physicians, Dr. Robin Warren and Dr. Barry Marshall, identified a link between *H. pylori* bacteria and peptic ulcers. Drs. Warren and Marshall had difficulty getting the medical community to acknowledge their discovery, and in 1995 most physicians in the U.S. still treated ulcers as if they were caused only by stress. Physicians were treating only 5% of ulcer patients with antibiotics. It wasn't until Dr. Marshall induced ulcers in his own stomach by swallowing *H. pylori* that the theory was taken seriously. In 1997, the Center for Disease Control launched a campaign to educate physicians and change their attitudes about ulcers. In 2005, Marshall and Warren were awarded the Nobel Prize in Physiology or Medicine "for their discovery of the bacterium *Helicobacter pylori* and its role in gastritis and peptic ulcer disease" (Ahmen, 2005).

Research involves uncovering truths that may have previously been unknown. Research is a creative process (as is writing), which makes it a "messy" one that, at times, involves argument and debate. Thus, as you evaluate research, keep in mind the following quote from 19th century German philosopher Schopenhauer: "All truth passes through three stages: First, it is ridiculed. Second, it is violently opposed. Third, it is accepted as being self-evident" (1958).

Are there times when you have an insight, but no one can see what you see? Are there times when you don't listen because the message does not fit into your worldview?

Credible Sources

As you know, some online sources are not credible; for the most part, anyone can post anything on the Web. Readers must use discretion and be selective. To start, look for university-affiliated sites and the sites of credible institutions. For example, PubMed was developed by National Center for Biotechnology Information (NCBI) at the U.S. National Library of Medicine (NLM), located at the National Institutes of Health (NIH). When you use unfamiliar online sources, consider the following:

1. Does the site appear professional and current?

2. Is the purpose to inform or to persuade?
3. Is it a personal blog or professional organization?
4. How long has the site been in operation? How often is it updated?
5. Is the site linked to other sites you consider reputable?
6. Can you identify any bias?
7. Does the site contain ads? Is it profit driven?
8. Who is the audience? Is it intended for experts in the field or a general audience?
9. Is the site tied to a private corporation or non-profit organization? If so, have you checked the accuracy of the information through academic sites?

When you evaluate any source, consider the following:

1. Who is the author, and what are their credentials?
2. Who is providing the funding?
3. Has the author written other publications on the topic? Have they written on other topics? (Do an online search.)
4. Is the author associated with a group or does the author have an agenda that is personal, political, social, or otherwise?
5. Who is the intended audience? Is it for scholars or a general audience?
6. Have others referenced this source?
7. Is the data verifiable and accurate?
8. Who published the article and when? Do the publishers have an editorial position?
9. Was it peer reviewed? If self-published, were there outside editors or reviewers?
10. What are the research citations? When was the research published?
11. Are the sources primary or secondary?

It is important to consider whether a source you are citing is a *primary source* or a *secondary source*. Primary sources include autobiographies, letters, diary entries, photographs, public records, news film footage, and speeches. Secondary sources provide interpretation and analysis of primary sources and include biographies, analyses, and critiques. While primary sources stay fresh, secondary sources may become dated; use the most relevant and recent sources, and evaluate each source on a case by case basis (University of Guelph, 2022).

Here are some tips for selecting good sources:

1. If you use a site such as Wikipedia, which can be helpful as an overview, also examine and read the original documentation that supports what is stated. Cite original documentation in your research, not Wikipedia.
2. Use .org sites to better understand advocacy and evaluate whether their data provides evidence only to support their cause or whether the data is evidence based and can be used in a broader context.
3. Be skeptical of for-profit sites as well as blogs and opinion sites (many of which end in ".com"). Evaluate whether information is based on evidence; if so, evaluate whether the evidence is reliable.
4. Use sources your library has already screened before you put your topic into an outside search engine. (Your library has screened many sources through online subscriptions to data bases.)
5. Compare how information on a website meshes with the print materials in your research. (Since print materials are scrutinized heavily during the publishing process, online sources that validate those sources can be considered more seriously.)
6. If you have a question, discuss your source with your local librarian.

ANALYZING YOUR RESEARCH

Think of the last journal article that you read:

- Did it discuss quantitative research, qualitative research, or both?
- Did you agree with the findings?
- Did you find flaws in how the research was conducted or fallacies in the author's conclusions?
- How did the research help shape your thinking?

Though you may start your research online, use your online sampling as an entrée to books and periodicals that provide substance and balance. What your library does not carry in hard copy or online subscriptions, it may carry in the form of microfilm or microfiche. Libraries can also request material for you through inter-library loan—one more reason to start your research early.

Bias and Fraud

The primary reason to identify credible sources is to avoid bias, which is not easy to identify. In addition, fraud is not easy to identify either. As a result, much research data cannot be taken at face value. The most powerful determinant of bias and fraud is a profit motive. A recent example can be found in the multibillion-dollar corporation Theranos, which was exposed for fraudulent claims and whose CEO was indicted for fraud (Allyn, 2022).

As part of your process, identify whether the authors of research promote perspectives from which they can benefit. If you find that is the case, compare outcomes of several studies by different sources. In addition, can you identify your own biases? Professionals are expected to become aware of their own biases and manage them effectively. Also consider the following:

- Was the research properly designed?
- Based on the experimental design, could reporting bias be a factor?
- Who is funding the research?

Science is constantly evolving; as knowledge evolves over time, some theories fall to the wayside. Have you ever heard about research that was once considered valid but was later revealed to be inaccurate or invalid?

Displaying Research

When you turn complicated data into charts, graphs, or tables, the relations between concepts and numbers can become apparent at a glance. APA provides extensive information on charts, graphs, and tables, so consider the information here an introduction. When you are deep into advanced research, refer directly to the *Publication Manual of the American Psychological Association* (2020b) for finer details on displaying your research most effectively.

To create graphs and charts, you can use various programs, such as Word, Excel, PowerPoint, Photoshop, and Illustrator. To become familiar with what these programs can do for you, perform the following internet search: "how to create graphs and charts in [list program]." As you watch the tutorials, take notes, and identify which applications would work best with your data.

Labeling and Placing Graphics

For each graphic you use in your paper, create a *callout* (e.g., "See Figure 1," "Table 2 shows …," and so on). When you refer to a graphic in your paper, use the page number on which it appears (unless the figure immediately follows the callout); and a brief descriptor, such as "Table 1 on page 13 includes data … ." In other words, don't use statements such as "in the table below," as this could make it more difficult for the reader to locate the graphic (APA, 2020, p. 197).

You can either integrate graphics into the body of your paper or place them at the end of your paper after the reference page. You can also create an appendix that contains the graphics and a brief description of each. Be sure to align graphics with the left margin, and if you are placing graphics within your paper, position them after full paragraphs.

Graphics: Charts, Graphs, and Tables

Visual displays can instantly illuminate meaning, patterns, and trends, which is why they can be more effective than descriptions that include explanations interspersed with numbers (WPTD Staff, 2020).

Charts provide a general picture, showing relationships between different data sets as well as patterns and trends. Since readers can gain insight at a glance, charts are more effective for presentations and videos. *Pie charts* show relative proportions of time or resources, *bar charts* show distributions of results, *scatter charts* can be used to show the relationship between two sets of data, and *line graphs* are used to show trends over a period of time.

Tables offer more specific detail. Since readers need time to analyze information in a table, tables are effective in printed materials. Tables should be used instead of charts when precision is key, such as for scientific or medical research reporting.

Bar Charts

Use a bar chart to compare and contrast (see Figure 6.3). You can show relationships over a period of time by clustering several different groups in the chart. The following guidelines apply to any type of bar chart:

- Display relationships horizontally or vertically.
- Make sure bar widths and the space between them is equal.

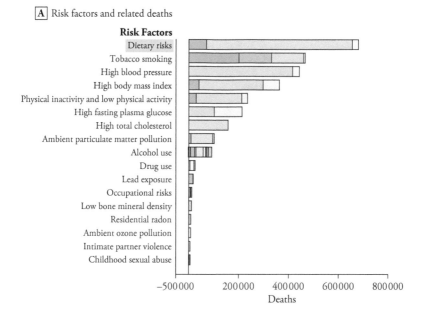

FIGURE 6.3   Number of Deaths and Percentage of Disability-Adjusted Life-Years Related to the 17 Leading Risk Factors in the United States in 2010 for Both Sexes Combined

- Arrange bars in a logical order (e.g., by length, age, or date) to make comparisons simpler.

Pie Charts

Use pie charts when the various components add up to 100% (see Figure 6.4). Follow these guidelines when creating a pie chart:

- Limit the number of categories; if you have more than eight, try to combine them.
- Label categories directly, and add percentages.
- Place the most important section at the 12 o'clock position to emphasize a point.

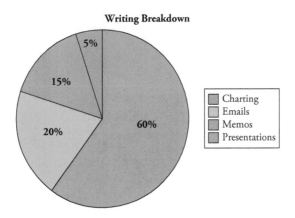

Writing Breakdown

5%

15%

20%

60%

Charting
Emails
Memos
Presentations

FIGURE 6.4   Professional Writing as a Nurse: A Writing Breakdown

Most of the writing is done through documentation and charting, which involves more short notes and checking boxes on a screen.

Scatter Charts

A scatter chart is also called a *scatter plot*. This type of chart reveals relationships between variables in a unique and important way. Scatter charts are versatile, giving insight into data that might otherwise seem confusing (TIBCO, 2022).

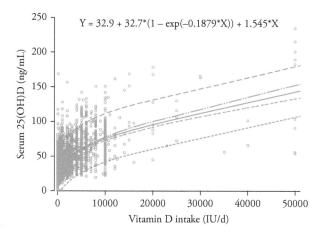

FIGURE 6.5   Scatter Graph of Vitamin D Supplementation

Tables

Tables should have enough information for readers to be able to inter-pret findings without explanation (see Figure 6.6). Use a table if you have data that needs to be analyzed in detail. If the reader needs to look at specific values or when precision is more important than trends or patterns, a table may be the best choice.

VAS	Sesame group (n = 22)	Control group (n = 23)	P†
Before	9.5	9	0.715
After	3.5	7	0.004

Conclusions: The present study showed a positive effect of sesame in improving clinical signs and symptoms in patients with knee OA and indicated that sesame might be a viable adjunctive therapy in treating OA.

FIGURE 6.6   Sesame Seeds for Knee Osteoarthritis

Line Graphs

Line graphs are used for quantitative date collected for a subject over a specified time interval; use line graphs to show trends.

- Use left-justified, 10- or 12-point, bold font for line graph titles.
- State what data the graph illustrates.
- Label each axis clearly.
- In a time graph, indicate time on the horizontal axis, and display units of measurement on the vertical axis.

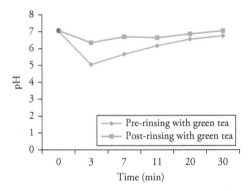

FIGURE 6.7   **Benefits of Using Green Tea as a Mouthwash to Prevent Plaque Build-up**

Recap

For some people, research is the most exciting aspect of their work and life. Even if you do not reach that point, you may find that research adds direction and power to making decisions or forming an argument. Good research applied the right way enriches life and helps alleviate human suffering.

WRITING WORKSHOP

Part I: Research Strengths and Weaknesses: Process Message

Instructions: After discussing the following questions with your peers, write a process message for your professor, sharing some of your insights. Even the best research has limitations. With a partner, analyze the "bigger picture." What are some of the strengths and weaknesses of how research is used and interpreted? Here are a few questions to get you started:

- What are the benefits of valid, unbiased research?
- Can you take the results of all research at "face value"? Why, or why not?
- What are some ways research design can produce biased results?
- Does practice keep up with evidence? How long does it take for the results of evidence-based research to be applied in your field of study?
- Are there times when professionals are so attached to past research that they close their mind to new understandings?

Part 2: The Research Interview

Instructions: Examine how decisions are made in your chosen field of study and the role that research plays by conducting a research interview with a professional in your future career. After your research interview, write a three- to five-page paper summarizing your results. Format your paper in APA style.

In your interview, explore the kinds of research your chosen professional does, the amount of time spent reviewing research, and other relevant information. To enhance your paper and add context to your findings, include an article related to your topic. (Make sure to include complete reference information on your reference page.)

Your interview may be conducted over the phone or in person. Let your interviewee know that it may take 20 to 30 minutes. While conducting the interview, collect data you can use to construct a table, chart, or graph. Therefore, as you plan your interview, analyze elements about the job that you can quantify.

Following is a list of questions you may use during the interview; however, feel free to add to these:

1. What is your position, and how long have you held it?
2. What kinds of problems do you address in your day-to-day operations?
3. What role does research play in your profession? What kinds of research do you review or apply in your field?

4. Are you required to do research? If so, what kind?

5. How heavily do you rely on research?

6. Do you use visuals for documents or presentations?

7. Do you feel you were adequately prepared by your education to do your work?

8. If you could give one piece of advice, what would it be?

Requirements

- Format your report in APA style, and include the following parts:
  - title page
  - abstract (just for the practice, if your professor requires it)
  - reference page (a reference page should only be included if you include a published article related to your topic)
  - a running head (if your professor requires it)
- In the opening paragraph, explain the purpose of the report, and introduce the person you have interviewed.
- In your conclusion, recap some of your insights. What did you learn about your future profession? What might you do differently as a result of what you learned?
- Format your interview summary in paragraphs, not in the question–answer format sometimes used for interviews.
- Include an original graphic—a chart, graph, or table—in your paper according to APA guidelines.
  - In Microsoft Word, options for making charts, graphs, and tables are available in the Insert tab located next to the Home tab. To create your visual, use data from your questions.
  - For assistance in creating a graphic, contact technical support at your university or search online for tutorials.
- APA citation style does not call for including a personal interview on a reference list because the interview cannot be retrieved and read; however, in-text citations should be included.

  narrative citation: J. Smith (personal communication, February 11, 2023)

parenthetical citation: (J. Smith, personal communication, February 11, 2023)

Since your entire paper uses information from only one interview, do not overcite. At the beginning of your paper, cite your interview once as a narrative citation and another time as a parenthetical citation. If you need clarification, check with your instructor.

References

Ahmed, N. (2005). 23 years of the discovery of *Helicobacter pylori*: Is the debate over? *Annals of Clinical Microbiology and Antimicrobials, 4*(17). https://doi.org/10.1186/1476-0711-4-17

Allyn, B. (January 3, 2022). *Elizabeth Holmes verdict: Former Theranos CEO found guilty on four counts.* NPR. Retrieved August 4, 2022, from https://www.npr.org/2022/01/03/1063973490/elizabeth-holmes-trial-verdict-guilty-theranos

American Psychological Association. (2020a). *Concise guide to APA style* (7th ed.). https://doi.org/10.1037/0000173-000, p. 13.

American Psychological Association. (2020b). *Publication manual of the American Psychological Association* (7th ed.). American Psychological Association. https://doi.org/10.1037/0000165-000

Awadalla H. I., Ragab M. H., Bassuoni M. W., Fayed M. T., Abbas M. O. (2011). A pilot study of the role of green tea use on oral health. *International Journal of Dental Hygiene, 9*(2),110–116. https://www.doi.org/10.1111/j.1601-5037.2009.00440.x.

Cornell University. (2022). *How to prepare an annotated bibliography.* https://guides.library.cornell.edu/annotatedbibliography

Dewey, J. (1967). *Democracy and education.* The Free Press.

Eftekhar, S. B., Khadem, H. M., Alipoor, B., Malek, M. A., Asghari, J. M., Moghaddam, A. (2013). Effects of sesame seed supplementation on clinical signs and symptoms in patients with knee osteoarthritis. *International Journal of Rheumatic Diseases, 16*(5), 578–582.

Ellis, M. (April 2022). *Professional writing as a nurse.* [Unpublished manuscript]. Professional Writing, Indiana University Northwest.

Garland, C., French, C., Baggerly, L., Heaney, R. (2011). Vitamin D supplement doses and serum 25-hydroxyvitamin D in the range associated with cancer prevention. *Anticancer Research, 31*(2):607–11.

Schopenhauer, A. (1958). Die welt als wille und vorstellung (E. F. J. Payne, Trans.). In *The world as will and representation* (Vol. I), Falcon's Wing Press. (Original work published 1818)

Streefkerk, R. (November 6, 2020). *APA Abstract (2020) | Formatting, Length, and Keywords.* Scribr. Retrieved April 30, 2022, from https://www.scribbr.com/apa-style/apa-abstract/

TIBCO. (November 11, 2022). *What is a scatter chart?* https://www.tibco.com/reference-center/what-is-a-scatter-chart. https://www.tibco.com/reference-center/what-is-a-scatter-chart

Tolson, T. (2019). *Treatments for depression in elderly patients.* Indiana University Northwest, Social Work Department.

University of Guelph. (2022). *Write clearly: Using evidence effectively.* https://guides.lib.uoguelph.ca/UseEvidenceEffectively

U.S. Burden of Disease Collaborators. (2013). The state of US health, 1990–2010: Burden of disease, injuries, and risk factors. *Journal of the American Medical Association, 310*(6), 591–608.

WPTD Staff. (September 1, 2020). *Charts vs tables or when to use one over the other.* wpData. https://wpdatatables.com/charts-vs-tables/

Writing Center, University of Wisconsin–Madison. (n.d.). *Writing an abstract for your research paper.* https://writing.wisc.edu/handbook/assignments/writing-an-abstract-for-your-research-paper/

Author Note: N. Casas, Assistant Librarian for Teaching and Learning, Indiana University, Northwest, contributed to this chapter.

Figure Credits

7

QUOTATION AND CITATION

While the *Publication Manual of the American Psychological Association* (2020) covers many topics, its primary purpose is providing a consistent and reliable citation system for crediting sources. Citation involves skill in knowing how to display quotation marks with punctuation as well as how to use ellipses, brackets, and parentheses, and this chapter assists you in learning those mechanics.

Citation provides the following benefits:

- Authors are acknowledged for their research and contributions to the field.
- Writers gain credibility for using published evidence to support their work. When research is published, a rigorous peer review process evaluates the quality of studies, identifying flaws and gaps as well as corroborating the value of the results.
- Readers can review the original source to gain additional depth and insight.

For all writing, but especially academic writing, the importance of citation cannot be overstated. However, a major issue involving citation is plagiarism. At times, developing writers inadvertently plagiarize, being uncertain about how to cite sources correctly or lacking an understanding of what plagiarism is. At other times, college students plagiarize on purpose. In fact, an informal poll conducted in 2007 revealed that 60.8% of college students who responded admitted to cheating (Open Education Database, 2018). In addition, of those polled, 16.5% of those who plagiarized felt no guilt for doing so. Plagiarists justify their actions, in part, because higher grades lead to more "success."

Before taking plagiarism lightly, consider the following:

> Psychologists at the University of British Columbia found that students who cheated in high school and college were likely to meet the criteria for psychopathic personality ... . The researchers found that academic cheaters also scored high in two other personality traits: narcissism (people who suffer from grandiosity, self-centeredness and an outsized sense of entitlement) and Machiavellianism (cynical, amoral types who make it a habit to manipulate others). But of the three disordered personalities ... psychopathy was the only trait significantly associated with student cheating. (Song, 2010)

Also, according to Garrett et al. (2016), the first time a person lies or cheats is the most difficult, with subsequent attempts becoming easier; this type of behavior can even snowball over time, leading to quite large crimes. Thus, when writers intentionally plagiarize, the sooner they break the cycle, the better.

If you would like to learn more about the causes of and cures for plagiarism, resources, such as plagiarism.org, are available. While citation can be intimidating at first, building skill also builds confidence, an effective antidote to plagiarism.

When you complete this chapter, you will

- be able to apply closed punctuation style with quotation marks,
- be able to use single quotation marks for quotations that appear within quotations,
- be able to identify long quotations and format them correctly,
- be able to use proper spacing with ellipses, parentheses, and brackets, and
- understand the basics of narrative and parenthetical citation as well as how to format a reference page.

Quotations

Quotations placed in exactly the right place add credibility and energy to your writing; however, use quotations and paraphrases sparingly and only as evidence to support your theses. Developing your own voice is neither mystery nor magic but a matter of practice. The more you write from your own understanding, the stronger your voice becomes.

Quotation Marks

While there are two types of quotation marks, double (") and single ('), APA follows the American English convention, with single quotation marks being used rarely and only for specific purposes. Thus, for our purposes, "quotation marks" refers to double marks. Single quotation marks are discussed later in this chapter in the "Quotations Within Quotations" section. (In short, use single quotation marks only when you are quoting within a quote.)

Quotation marks are an important element of citation, but they are used for other purposes as well. Here are the primary reasons for using quotation marks:

1. inserting a direct quote of three or fewer lines within the body of a document
2. setting off the title of a book chapter or article in the body of text
3. identifying technical terms or coined expressions that may be unfamiliar
4. using words humorously or ironically
5. showing a slang expression or an intentionally misused word
6. referring to "a letter, word, phrase, or sentence as a linguistic example" (APA, 2020, p. 157), for example:

   The word "listen" has several shades of meaning.

However, do not use quotation marks to make a word stand out, as using quotation marks will imply the opposite. For example, in the following, your reader may assume that you are being sarcastic:

That's a "great" idea.

In the following instances you should use italics rather than quotation marks:

- to stress a word
- to highlight a key term for which you are providing a definition

To avoid overuse of quotation marks, follow this advice: When in doubt, leave quotations out.

Quotation Marks: Closed Style vs. Open Style

Writers are sometimes confused about the correct way to display quotation marks (i.e., whether quotation marks should be on the inside or the outside of a period). The confusion remains in part because there are two basic ways to display quotation marks: the *closed style* and the *open style*:

- **closed style:** Place quotation marks on the outside of commas and periods.

  "Thank you."

- **open style:** Place quotation marks on the inside of commas and periods.

  "You are welcome".

American English uses closed style, while British English uses open style. Thus, for APA, use closed style. (In fact, throughout your studies in American universities, also use closed style.)

Quotation Marks with Punctuation

When using quotation marks, make sure to display them correctly in conjunction with commas, periods, semicolons, and colons. When applying closed punctuation style, here are some rules to remember:

1. Commas and periods are placed inside quotation marks.

   In Chapter 1, "On Courage," Kohut discusses human behavior in times of crisis (Kohut, 1985).

2. Semicolons and colons are placed on the outside of quotation marks.

   The doctor emphasized, "Take the medication immediately"; the patient complied.

3. The placement of *question marks* depends on the meaning. That is, does the quotation itself pose a question, or is the quotation within a sentence that poses the question. (The same pattern is followed for *exclamation points.*)

   Was it Mies van der Rohe who said, "Less is more"?

   Robert Browning asked, "For all types of writing, is less more?"

4. Place footnotes and endnotes directly on the outside of quotation marks (no space added).

   According to the Infectious Disease Clinics (2018), the virus can spread quickly: "Insects, birds and some species of animal are carriers."[3]

While footnotes can be used for APA style to provide additional information or copyright information, they are more frequently used for Modern Library Association (MLA) style and the *Chicago Manual of Style* (*CMoS*). Also, for APA style, in-text citation is used, so you would need to use a parenthetical citation for the page number.

5. Never double punctuate at the end of a sentence:

   incorrect: They included the question, "How many participants completed the study?".

   correct: They included the question, "How many participants completed the study?"

Short Quotations

Incorporate direct quotes that include fewer than 40 words into your narrative, and set them off by using quotation marks. For *in-text* and *parenthetical citations*, place the citation outside of the closing quotation mark, and then place the period outside of the parenthesis

> According to Galanis et al. (2021), "Of the 16 studies, the overall prevalence of emotional exhaustion was 34.1%, and the increased workload and lower level of specialized training was a main risk factor" (p. 19).

> For the training, some of the scenarios included "maternal simulation, newborn simulation, and computer-based documentation with case scenarios" (Febbraro & Arnold, 2012, p. 82).

When a quotation is a complete sentence, capitalize the first word, regardless of where the quote starts in the sentence.

Block Quotations

Long quotations of forty or more words are called *block quotations*. Display these quotations separately from the text by doing the following:

- Indent the quote 0.5 inches from the left margin. (Do not use quotation marks; the indentation signals the quote.)
- In APA style, double space the quotation.
- Place the period at the end of the quote, not at the end of the citation.

> Although beginning practitioners often think that methods, approaches, or skills are the critical factors in achieving good client outcomes, clients surveyed in many research studies reported that the relationship qualities of warmth, respect, genuineness, empathy, and acceptance were most important. (Chang et al., 2009, p. 72)

Quotations Within Quotations

As previously mentioned, there are two types of quotation marks: single and double. For American English, single quotation marks should be used for a quote within a quote.

For short quotes (fewer than 40 words of quoted material):

- Display the main quote between double quotation marks.
- Display the internal quote with single quotation marks.

> According to Kegan (1983), "Carl Rogers's 'client-centered' or 'nondirective' therapy has had an enormous influence on the training and practice of three generations of counselors and therapists" (p. 302).

> According to Cummins et al. (2011), "Long-time policy practitioners realize that 'it is really all about relationship'" (p. 19).

Indirect Quotes or Paraphrasing

When you paraphrase, you express an author's ideas in your own words and should not use quotation marks. However, you must credit the source by using the author's last name and date. Following is a paraphrase of the quote from a previous example by Chang et al.

> According to Chang et al. (2009), establishing an empathetic, respectful, and authentic relationship between the client and practitioner was the most important factor in achieving good outcomes.

Brackets for Changing or Adding Words in Quotations

At times, you must change or add a word or two to quoted material so that the reader can make sense of the quote in its new context. When you add a word or two of your own, put the new text between brackets.

> Jones (2012) asked what "knowledge, skills, and values [were] necessary for culturally competent service provision" (p. 3).

Ellipses for Omitting Words in Quotations

An ellipsis mark consists of three spaced periods; these can either be spaced manually or made using your word processor's automatically created ellipsis character. Use ellipses to show omission of a word or words from a quote. If the omission comes at the end of a sentence of quoted material, add one more period to indicate the end of the sentence, as in the following example.

According to Greger (2015),

> Legume consumption is associated with a slimmer waist and lower blood pressure, and randomized trials have shown it can match or beat out calorie cutting for slimming tummy fat as well as improving the regulation of blood sugar, insulin levels and cholesterol … which may help reduce the risk of stroke, depression, and colon cancer. (p. 287)

Since ellipses are used for more than just omitting words in quotations, they are discussed in more detail in the following section.

Ellipses

"Ellipses" is the plural form of "ellipsis." Ellipses inform the reader that you are leaving out information. Since ellipses indicate that information is missing, their use removes an otherwise awkward gap.

In formal documents, ellipses allow writers to adapt quotations by leaving out less relevant information, making the main idea stand out. In informal documents, ellipses allow writers to jump from one idea to another, without entirely completing their thoughts. Ellipses also allow the writer to convey a sense of uncertainty without coming right out and stating it.

Consider the following when using an ellipsis mark:

- Ellipses consist of three periods (or dots) with a space before, between, and after each one.

  fully spaced ellipses: This doesn't make sense to me . . . so let me know what you think.

- Most software programs create ellipses when you space once, type three periods in a row, and then space once again, as follows:

  partially spaced ellipses: The meeting ended abruptly … and we will discuss it later.

- A fourth period is used when the missing information is at the end of the sentence in a formal quotation; however, APA (2020) recommends the following:

Do not use an ellipsis at the beginning or end of any quotation unless the original source includes an ellipsis; start or end the quotation at the point where the source's text begins or ends. Use four periods—that is, a period plus an ellipsis (. ...)—to show a sentence break within omitted material. (p. 275)

APA accepts both styles of ellipsis marks: the computer-generated (partially spaced style) and the spaced style. However, the preferred style for most academic and legal documents is the spaced ellipses, which is the traditional style. Whichever style you select, use ellipses sparingly, but correctly, even in informal use.

Parentheses

Parentheses are used for various reasons, with in-text citation being only one of them. Here are other reasons for using parentheses:

- to give a brief explanation within a sentence
- to insert a sentence that does not directly relate to the topic of your paragraph
- to supply abbreviations
- to set off letters and numbers used for lists within a sentence
- to display mathematical expressions
- to display phone numbers

In a narrative, using parentheses deemphasizes information. Parentheses also help to break up information flow in a positive way; parentheses tell the reader that the information is related to the broader topic, without an explanation of how or why. By enclosing a few words in parentheses, you can sometimes avoid writing a lengthy explanation.

When you use parentheses, type them correctly by including a space before the first parenthesis and after the last one.

incorrect: My number is (312)555-5555.

correct: My number is (312) 555-5555.

incorrect: Johansen (2010) reported that the data was incomplete.

correct: Johansen (2010) reported that the data was incomplete.

incorrect: The study correlated nutritional habits with types of disease(Gerard, 2016).

correct: The study revealed some causes of homelessness (Gerard, 2016).

Citation

Though details about citation have been covered in previous chapters, here is a review of basic information about in-text citation and references.

In-Text Citation

In-text citation refers to author–date references in the body of the text.

- A narrative citation uses an author's name in the text of the writing (not in parentheses). At times, the writer also includes the year in the text. As the term implies, narrative citations are embedded in the narrative.

  example: Quinlan (2020) conducted the original research.

  example: In 2020, Quinlan conducted the original research.

- A parenthetical citation includes all citation information in parentheses and often occurs at the end of a sentence (but not always). As the term implies, parenthetical citations are not part of the flow of the sentence but interjected as reference information.

  example: The original research did not include a control group (Quinlan, 2020).

  example: The original research did not include a control group (Quinlan, 2020); however, subsequent trials have included control groups (Martinez, 2021; Yeung, 2022).

- Place the parenthetical citation within the sentence; in other words, place the period on the outside of the right parenthesis.

While you may find in-text citation challenging at first; by embracing the style, you will quickly adapt to it.

SENTENCE PROMPTS FOR ACADEMIC WRITING

To adapt to in-text citation, you must also adapt your writing style. One way to coach yourself is using sentence prompts to structure your ideas. The University of Manchester's "Academic Phrasebank" can help ease you into building your academic vocabulary, covering extensive examples for discussing the following:

- being cautious
- being critical
- classifying and listing
- comparing and contrasting
- defining terms
- describing trends

- describing quantities
- explaining causality
- giving examples
- signaling transition
- writing about the past ("Academic Phrasebank," n.d.)

Take the following example from the phrasebank:

Redgrave (2018)	observed	significant	differences between x and y.
	reported	considerable	
	described	only slight	
	studied	major	

When you are at a loss for finding the right words, take time to nourish your vocabulary, reviewing examples that serve as models for academic and scientific writing. As you build your understanding, you are also building your confidence.

Narrative and Parenthetical Citations

Following are additional examples of in-text citations:

- For narrative citations, follow authors' names with the publication year in parentheses.

  Ornish (1992) published research demonstrating that diet could reverse heart disease.

- For parenthetical citations, enclose authors' names and year of publication in parentheses at the end of the sentence.

  When patients increased consumption of fruits and vegetables, weight and blood pressure reduced significantly (Barnard, 2019; Klaper, 2020).

- When the authors' names and publication year are part of the part of the narrative, that is sufficient.

  In 2015, Kempner and McDougall studied insulin resistance in a fat-rich diet.

  For subsequent narrative citation within the same paragraph, the date is not necessary. (However, use the date for all parenthetical citations.)

  When patients increased consumption of fruits and vegetables, weight and blood pressure reduced significantly (Barnard, 2019; Klaper, 2020). Barnard further states that the reduction in blood pressure has a multitude of additional long-term health benefits.

- When a work has two authors, cite both names each time they are referenced:

  McMartin and Yeung (2014) concluded that mental health and diet are associated.

- When a work has three or more authors, use only the surname of the first author followed by "et al." (But do not use "et al." on the reference page.)

  Esselsten et al. (2018) demonstrated additional research was warranted.

- For quotations longer than 40 words, indent the left margin 0.5 inches, do not use quotation marks, and place the reference outside of the period of the last sentence.

> The two most prominent dietary risks for death and disability in the world may be not eating enough fruit and eating too much salt. … Sodium is an essential nutrient, but vegetables and other natural foods provide the small amounts of sodium you need in your diet. (Greger, 2015, p. 124)

- For short quotations, place the reference inside of the period:

> "Additional studies are needed to fill the gap" (Jones, 2010, p. 33).

Reference Page

In APA style, title the reference page "References" (not "Resources," "Bibliography," or "Works Cited"). Use the following conventions on your reference page:

- Type the title of the reference page at the top of the page (in other words, don't space down).
- Double space the reference page, and use the same font as used in the body of the paper.
- Use hanging indentation style, with second lines indented 0.5 inches (set your controls in the Paragraph tab in your toolbar).

In addition, if you use a citation generator, do not simply copy and paste the information on the reference page. Citation generators are created using a computer algorithm, and capitalization, parentheses, and other elements may be erroneous. Therefore, make sure to edit the citation so that it is displayed in hanging indentation style, double spaced, with the correct font style and size. Refer to the following guidelines when creating your reference list:

- List the references in alphabetical order, leaving individual references in the order noted in the article or book.
- Use the author's last name and first initial; list all authors if there are 20 or fewer (do not use "et al." in the reference list).

- For 21 or more authors, include the names of the first 19 authors, insert an ellipsis, and then add the final author's name (do not use an ampersand).
- Align the first line of each reference with the left margin. Indent subsequent lines 0.5 inches (using hanging indentation).
- Present the title of a book and an article in sentence case; present the title of a journal in title case.
  - **sentence case:** Capitalize only the first word of the title, the first word after a colon (subtitle), and proper nouns and proper adjectives.
  - **title case:** Type titles in uppercase and lowercase letters, following basic guidelines for capitalization.
- Italicize the titles of books and journal articles (including the journal's volume number).
- Include digital object identifiers (DOIs) and URLs, if available.
- For books, include the author's last name and initials, publication date, title of work, and publisher.

Titus, S., & Barker, D. (2012). *Title in sentence case.* Publisher.

- For information sourced from a webpage, include a retrieval date if the website is designed to change over time.

Jones, S., & Barker, D. (2012). *Title in sentence case.* Retrieved May 29, 2021, from http://www.websitename.com/complete-url

- When the author and publisher are the same, omit the publisher from the reference.

Recap

You now have a basic understanding of how to display quoted material and integrate narrative and parenthetical citations into your writing. When you are compiling complicated references, seek out specific details by referring to the *Publication Manual of the American Psychological Association*, 7th edition (2020).

WRITING WORKSHOP

Part 1: Narrative and Parenthetical Citations

Instructions: Place the following quotations in sentences, using a narrative and a parenthetical in-text citation for each. Since the quotations are taken out of context, you will need to use a "lead-in" phrase, such as the following:

● According to Author x and Author y, …

● According to Author et al., there is …

The goal of this exercise is to practice using quotations in sentences and citing them correctly. Review the following example before moving on to the numbered exercises.

quote: "learners actively participate and achieve better conceptual learning as compared to other traditional lecture methods"

source: S. F. Ajmal & M. Hafeez, p. 129

date: 2021

narrative style: According to Ajmal and Hafeez (2021), "Learners actively participate and achieve better conceptual learning as compared to other traditional lecture methods" (p. 129).

parenthetical style: "Learners actively participate and achieve better conceptual learning as compared to other traditional lecture methods" (Ajmal & Hafeez, 2021 p. 129).

1. **quote:** "students are able to cover course material at a pace that agrees with their learning style"

   source: A. S. Burke, & B. Fedorek, p. 14

   date: 2021

   narrative style:

   parenthetical style:

2. **quote:** "being responsible for one's own learning is both a key 21st-century employment-related skill and critical to the success of the flipped classroom"

   source: R. L. Fisher, R. LaFerrier, & A. Rixon, p. 548

   date: 2020

   narrative style:

   parenthetical style:

3. **quote:** "very little and inconclusive evidence that flipped learning improves student outcomes or 21st-century employability skills"

   source: Fisher, R. L., LaFerrier, R., & Rixon, A., p. 543

   date: 2020

   narrative style:

   parenthetical style:

4. **quote:** Flipped learning is "well-suited to heutagogy, where the learner is responsible for their self-directed learning and in so doing develops the skills of lifelong learning"

   source: L. M. Blaschke, p. 56

   date: 2012

   narrative style:

   parenthetical style:

5. **quote:** "no significant statistical difference in student learning outcomes"

   source: S. F. Ajmal, & M. Hafeez, p. 128

   date: 2021

   narrative style:

   parenthetical style:

Part 2: Reference List

Instructions: Format the following reference entries in correct APA style. Here are some prompts to get you started:

- What type of indentation style is used for references?

- How should the authors' names be formatted?
- For any of the references, do you need a "retrieved from" date? (If so, use today's date.)
- Should some information be in italics?
- What is the correct order for the references, and why?

Ajmal, S. F. and Hafeez, M., 2021, Critical Review on Flipped Classroom model versus Traditional Lecture Method. International-al Journal of Education, 9(1), 128-140. https://doi:10.18488/journal.61.2021.91.128.140

L. M. Blaschke, (2012), Heutagogy And Lifelong Learning: a review of Heutagogical practice and self-determined learning. The International Review of Research in Open and Distributed Learning, 13, 56-71.

Burke, A. S. & Fedorek, B., (2017). Does "flipping" promote engagement?: a comparison of a traditional, online, and flipped class. Active Learning in Higher Education, 18(1), 11-24. https:doi/10.1177/1469787417693487

R. L. Fisher, LaFerriere, R., and Rixon, A., (2020), Flipped Learning: an effective Pedagogy with an Achilles' heel. Innovations in Education and Teaching International 57(5). 543-554. https://doi.org/10.1080/14703297.2019.1635904

EXERCISE KEYS

Part 1: Narrative and Parenthetical Citations

Note: Answers may vary.

1. **Quote:** "students are able to cover course material at a pace that agrees with their learning style"

   Source: A. S. Burke & B. Fedorek, page 14

   Date: 2021

   Narrative Style: According to Burke and Fedorek (2021), "Students are able to cover course material at a pace that agrees with their learning style" (p. 14).

Parenthetical Style: "Students are able to cover course material at a pace that agrees with their learning style" (Burke & Fedorek, 2021, p. 14).

2. **Quote:** "being responsible for one's own learning is both a key twenty-first-century employment-related skill and critical to the success of the flipped classroom"

Source: R. L. Fisher. R. LaFerrier & A. Rixon, p. 548

Date: 2020

Narrative Style: As stated by Fisher et al. (2020), "Being responsible for one's own learning is both a key twenty-first-century employment-related skill and critical to the success of the flipped classroom" (p. 548).

Parenthetical Style: "Being responsible for one's own learning is both a key twenty-first-century employment-related skill and critical to the success of the flipped classroom" (Fisher et al., 2020, p. 548).

3. **Quote:** "very little and inconclusive evidence that flipped learning improves student outcomes or 21st-century employability skills"

Source: Fisher, R. L., LaFerrier, R., & Rixon, A., p. 543

Date: 2020

Narrative Style: According to Fisher et al. (2020), there is "very little and inconclusive evidence that flipped learning improves student outcomes or 21st-century employability skills" (p. 543).

Parenthetical Style: There is "very little and inconclusive evidence that flipped learning improves student outcomes or 21st-century employability skills" (Fisher et al., 2020, p. 543).

4. **Quote:** Flipped learning is "well-suited to heutagogy, where the learner is responsible for their self-directed learning and in so doing develops the skills of lifelong learning"

Source: L. M. Blaschke, page 56

Date: 2012

Narrative Style: According to Blascheke (2012), flipped learning is "well-suited to heutagogy, where the learner is responsible for their self-directed learning and in so doing develops the skills of lifelong learning" (p. 56).

Parenthetical Style: Flipped learning is "well-suited to heutagogy, where the learner is responsible for their self-directed learning and in so doing develops the skills of lifelong learning" (Blaschke, 2012, p. 56).

5. **Quote:** "no significant statistical difference in student learning outcomes"

Source: Ajmal, S. F., Hafeez, M., p. 128

Date: 2021

Narrative Style: According to Ajmal and Hafeeze (2021), there is "no significant statistical difference in student learning outcomes" (p. 128).

Parenthetical Style: There is "no significant statistical difference in student learning outcomes" (Ajmal & Hafeez, 2021, p. 128).

Part 2: Reference List

Ajmal, S. F. & Hafeez, M. (2021). Critical review on flipped classroom model versus traditional lecture method. *International Journal of Education, 9*(1), 128-140. Retrieved August 3, 2022, from https://doi:10.18488/journal.61.2021.91.128.140

Blaschke, L. M. (2012). Heutagogy and lifelong learning: A review of heutagogical practice and self-determined learning. *The International Review of Research in Open and Distributed Learning, 13*, 56-71.

Burke, A. S. & Fedorek, B. (2017). Does "flipping" promote engagement?: A comparison of a traditional, online, and flipped class. *Active Learning in Higher Education, 18*(1), 11-24. Retrieved August 3, 2022, from https: doi/10.1177/1469787417693487

Fisher, R. L., LaFerriere, R., & Rixon, A. (2020). Flipped learning: An effective pedagogy with an Achilles' heel. *Innovations in Education and Teaching International 57*(5). 543-554. Retrieved August 3, 2022, from https://doi.org/10.1080/14703297.2019.1635904

Note. Adapted from "Strategy Review," by Galocy, L., 2021.

References

American Psychological Association. (2020). *Publication manual of the American Psychological Association* (7th ed.). https://doi.org/10.1037/0000165-000

Garrett, N., Lazzaro, S. C., Ariela, D., & Sharot, T. (2016). The brain adapts to dishonesty. *Nature Neuroscience, 19*, 1727–1732.

Greger, M. (2015). *How not to die.* Flat Iron Books.

Open Education Database. (2022). *8 astonishing stats on academic cheating.* Retrieved May 20, 2018, from https://oedb.org/ilibrarian/8-astonishing-stats-on-academic-cheating/

Song, S. (2010). *Profiling student cheaters: Are they psychopaths?* Retrieved May 21, 2018, from https://healthland.time.com/2010/09/20/profiling-student-cheaters-are-they-psychopaths/

University of Manchester. (n.d.). *Academic phrasebank.* Retrieved June 6, 2022, from http://www.phrasebank.manchester.ac.uk/

Author Note: N. Casas, Assistant Librarian for Teaching and Learning, Indiana University Northwest, and M. Ellis, BSN major at Indiana University Northwest, contributed to this chapter.

8

EFFECTIVE SENTENCES AND COHESIVE PARAGRAPHS

Though APA does not list specific requirements for writing effective sentences and paragraphs, the quality of your writing depends on your ability to do so. For example, writing students often complain that they write long and unfocused paragraphs, jumping from idea to idea. This chapter focuses on writing clear, concise sentences and paragraphs that are cohesive and focus on one topic.

Readers can see at a glance if writing is broken into effective chunks; and when they see paragraphs that seem to go on forever, they feel a sense of dread. In addition, when they read long, overly complicated sentences, they struggle to find meaning and may even lose interest. A few basic principles for editing sentences and paragraphs can assist you in bringing the quality of your writing to a level that is reader friendly, clear, and engaging.

As you gain more experience writing academic papers, you will appreciate the value of being able to control the structure of sentences and paragraphs. If you have not previously paid attention to editing sentences and paragraphs, now is the time to learn a few important principles.

When you complete this chapter, you will be able to

* control the structure, length, and content of sentences,

- develop cohesive and coherent paragraphs,
- build effective paragraphs by using a topic sentence and a topic string, and
- edit and revise sentences and paragraphs for effective information flow.

Developing effective paragraphs is a matter of editing: when you compose, write freely. When you edit, shape your writing for your reader. Let's start by reviewing guidelines for editing sentences and then paragraphs.

Sentences: Structure, Length, and Content

While APA (2020) recommends that sentences contain only one controlling idea, the manual does not take a stand on sentence length or structure. Let's review how those concepts contribute to writing reader friendly sentences that are clear in meaning.

Control Sentence Structure

To control sentence structure, focus on the sentence's core: the subject and verb. Together, the subject and verb convey meaning. If you have one without the other, meaning is incomplete. In fact, readers need to work harder to find meaning when the sentence core is presented ineffectively.

As you read the following example, notice your reaction:

Dr. Worthington, who is an expert in the field of health care and has worked with our department on several projects assisting our faculty and staff, will be our keynote speaker for this year's conference. (35 words)

Does the previous example sound wordy and confusing? Now read the following:

Dr. Worthington will be our keynote speaker during year's conference. Dr. Worthington is an expert in the field of health care and has worked with our department on several projects assisting our faculty and staff. (35 words)

Is the second example easier to understand? The difference between the two is that the second example broke the information into smaller chunks and used the sentence core effectively:

Dr. Worthington *will be* ...

Dr. Worthington *has worked* ...

In general, the closer the subject and verb are to each other, the easier it is for a reader to understand meaning. Here are some editing tips for presenting the sentence core effectively:

- Keep the subject and verb close to each other.
- Keep the sentence core close to the beginning of the sentence.

The sentence core is a critical unit for editing. When you form sentences with real subjects and strong verbs, you end up with effective sentences. (To learn more about real subjects and strong verbs, see Chapter 11.)

Control Sentence Length

Sentence length relates to the amount of information that the average reader retains. For example, beyond 25 words, a reader may find it necessary to reread the beginning of the sentence to understand its meaning. When you are writing about complicated topics, focus on sentence length when you edit:

> Writing experts suggest keeping sentences to fewer than 25 words in length because readers may have difficulty retaining information in longer sentences and may need to read the beginning of a sentence over again if the meaning of the beginning becomes lost by the time the end is reached. (49 words)

Excessively long sentences can become unmanageable for the reader but also for the writer. For example, the longer the sentence, the more demands is placed on keeping the grammar and punctuation correct. When you edit, identify excessively long sentences; either break the information into two shorter sentences or cut unnecessary information. If you choose to apply this guideline, you will sharpen your editing skills and improve the quality of your writing. Readers will also appreciate having easier access to your ideas.

Control Sentence Content

Each sentence should have only one controlling idea. When a sentence contains more than one controlling idea, the meaning is unclear:

> The Imminent Delivery Workshop trains nurses in the Emergency Department for unexpected labor and delivery, and many women come to our hospital to deliver.

In the previous sentence, ideas appear somewhat disjointed because each is given equal weight. You can correct this by showing how the ideas are related:

> Because many women come to our hospital to deliver, the Imminent Delivery Workshop trains nurses for unexpected labor and delivery in the Emergency Department.

Paragraphing: Process and Length

While the general guideline for sentence length is 25 words or fewer, a comparable suggestion for paragraph length is four to eight sentences. However, neither sentence length nor paragraph length are governed by rules; they abide by guidelines and suggestions.

While all sentences are not equal, neither are paragraphs. For example, a paragraph can be as short as a sentence or two—though APA advises against using single-sentence paragraphs whenever possible—or longer than eight sentences. When you make paragraph decisions, shape your writing for your reader with the intent of making ideas accessible. In part, the type of writing you are doing dictates the parameters and expectations for your paragraphs:

- **For academic papers,** paragraphs tend to be longer because ideas are developed in depth.
- **For professional writing,** such as e-mail, paragraphs are best kept short. E-mail messages tend to be conversational, and short paragraphs can stress important communications.

- **For blogs and other types of online writing,** short- to medium-length paragraphs catch and keep the reader's attention as well as convey ideas readily.

Academic writing, especially, is rife with examples of exceedingly long paragraphs. While paragraphs tend to be longer in academic papers than in other types of writing, paragraphs still need to be a reasonable length. When paragraphs are excessively long, readers lose their concentration and interest. Here is how to use paragraph length as a cue for editing:

1. **Count the number of sentences.** Keep most paragraphs between four and eight sentences. When a paragraph goes beyond eight sentences, see if you have shifted to a new topic and need to create a fresh paragraph.
2. **Do a word count.** If you keep paragraphs between 100 and 200 words, they remain manageable.
3. **Assess your writing at a glance.** If a paragraph goes beyond a half page, review the content to see if you have shifted topics, signaling the start of a new paragraph.
4. **Keep paragraph length proportional to the length of the paper.** For example, for shorter papers, aim for shorter paragraphs.

Once you develop skill with paragraphing, you will break your writing into paragraphs naturally as you compose and then refine them when you edit and revise. Read your writing out loud, or have someone read it to you. When you hear a new topic, start a new paragraph. By mixing up paragraph length, you add variety for the reader, which enhances attention and thus understanding. Short paragraphs grab the reader's attention, so use them when you want to add emphasis.

Cohesive and Coherent Paragraphs

As previously mentioned, effective paragraphs have two important qualities: they are cohesive and coherent. Cohesive paragraphs develop only one main idea or topic, demonstrating a connectedness among ideas that support that topic. Adequate details support the main idea, so the reader understands the main point. Coherent paragraphs develop the main idea through a logical flow of ideas—one point leads to the next.

To develop a cohesive paragraph, the first step when editing is identifying its *topic sentence*. A topic sentence gives an overview of the paragraph, and it contains broad and general information. The next step is ensuring that each sentence in the paragraph develops the topic, creating a *topic string*. A topic string is a series of sentences that develop the main idea of the topic sentence. Each sentence extends the controlling idea, providing specifics that illustrate the main idea of the topic sentence.

As you compose, do not be concerned about writing a topic sentence or building a topic string. In fact, you will gain clarity about your topic as you write about it, and you may often find that one of the later sentences in your draft paragraph becomes the topic sentence.

Here is a step-by-step process for editing paragraphs so that they are cohesive and coherent:

1. Identify the topic sentence. Select the sentence that develops the topic in a broad and general way.
2. Bring the topic sentence to the beginning of the paragraph as the first (or second) sentence.
3. Build a topic string with sentences that explain, expand, and support the topic sentence.
4. Cut sentences that do not fit, or use them to start a new paragraph.

Draft

Read the draft paragraph that follows. As you read the paragraph, ask yourself the following:

- What is the main topic? Which sentence expresses the main topic best?
- Which sentences seem off topic and belong in a different paragraph?

- How many different viewpoints are expressed? What are they?

> I believe that writing effective paragraphs is important, but I have always been unsure of where to make paragraph breaks. Now that I know that I can put my ideas down and then go back and edit, I think I can improve my writing if I take the time to read it over and make changes. Before I didn't take the time to edit paragraphs, now I do because I know how to use a topic sentence and create a topic string. Editing is an important part of the writing process. When you edit paragraphs, look for paragraphs that are long and then read them to see if you change topics. When you change topics, add a paragraph break. Then when you read the paragraph, look for the topic sentence. The topic sentence should be toward the beginning. The other thing about paragraphs is that all the sentences should be about the same topic. That's called a topic string. When there are ideas that are about different topics, those sentences should be cut, or they should be put in their own paragraph. When I read papers that jump from one topic to another, I get confused. Now I know that editing paragraphs can shape a confusing paper into one that makes sense. Take time to edit your paragraphs, and you will see an improvement in your writing.

Did the paragraph seem to ramble on, in part because of the changing topic?

Edited Version I

The following version focuses on how to edit but leaves out the writer's own experience; it is written in the "you" viewpoint:

> Editing paragraphs is an important part of the writing process. When you edit paragraphs, look for paragraphs that are long and then read them to see if you change topics. When you change topics, add a paragraph break. Move the topic sentence toward the beginning, and make sure all sentences are about the same topic. Cut sentences that don't belong. If you take time to edit, you will see an improvement in your writing.

Edited Version 2

Version 2 takes the writer's point of view. Notice how the voice shifts to the first-person "I" viewpoint:

> Writing effective paragraphs is important, but I have always been unsure of where to make paragraph breaks. Now that I know that I can put my ideas down and then go back and edit, I take the time to read it over and make changes. Before I didn't take the time to edit because I didn't know how to edit and revise paragraphs. I start by moving the topic sentence up front and then cutting what doesn't belong. When I take time to edit paragraphs, I see an improvement in my writing.

Edited Version 3

Version 3 uses the third-person point of view, giving it an academic tone:

> Editing paragraphs is an important part of the writing process. Editing involves shaping writing for the reader. For all types of writing, purpose is the most important element and should be placed at the beginning. The topic sentence should be placed toward the beginning of the paragraph, and information that does not support the topic sentence should be cut or moved to a new paragraph. The sentences related to the topic sentences create a topic string. When writers edit paragraphs effectively, their writing improves.

In academic writing, use the third-person viewpoint.

Information Flow

Information flow orders ideas, so readers understand how one idea relates to another:

- **Old information** is familiar information that provides a context for your reader.
- **New information** is unfamiliar information that extends the reader's understanding.

- **Empty information** is information that is irrelevant, redundant, or that does not add value.

In general, old information is the topic, and new information extends the reader's understanding of the topic. By placing *old information* (the topic) at the beginning of a sentence and *new information* at the end, writers create smoother transitions between ideas. By cutting *empty information*, meaning becomes clearer.

Coherent Paragraphs

To achieve a coherent paragraph, you are aiming for a logical flow of ideas; one idea leads logically to the next idea as it extends the reader's knowledge. To achieve a coherent paragraph, apply principles of information flow.

In each sentence, put old information first (the topic), and follow it with new information, extending the reader's understanding. An old-to-new information flow helps readers make connections; familiar ideas ease readers into the unfamiliar.

As you read the following paragraph, notice how the topic, "health program," appears in various locations of each sentence:

> *By implementing health and safety programs for employees*, a corporation can reap multiple rewards. Reduced absenteeism, increased productivity, and improved employee moral are often the results of *a comprehensive health program*. In addition, substantial savings in reduced insurance claims and premiums is another result of having *a health program*.

The paragraph sounds choppy because the writer presents new information first and then attaches it to "health program," which is old information. This cohesive paragraph can become coherent by adjusting the information flow; here's how:

- Move the topic "health and safety programs" (old information) to the beginning of each sentence.
- Move information about rewards (new information) to the end of each sentence.

Now, here is the same paragraph revised with an old-to-new information flow:

> By implementing health and safety programs for employees, a corporation can reap multiple rewards. A comprehensive occupational health program reduces absenteeism, increases productivity, and improves employee morale. In addition, a health program results in substantial savings by reducing insurance claims and premiums.

You may notice that the topic, "health and safety programs," changes subtly in its form, though not in its meaning. Varying form adds creativity and keeps writing from being monotonous.

Composing and Editing Paragraphs

When composing, do not concern yourself with writing cohesive, coherent paragraphs. Also, as you get your ideas on the page, don't be concerned about information flow; you may find yourself generating new information and then linking it to the old. You are still learning about your topic; organize and prioritize your ideas when you edit and revise.

For a paragraph to be coherent, ideas must flow logically. In other words, writing should not contain disjointed ideas. However, as you compose, disjointed ideas may seem to make sense. To edit the flow, step away from your work for a while, so you can evaluate your writing objectively.

Here are some tips for revising paragraphs:

- **Print out a copy.** Writing sometimes reads differently in hard copy than it does on the screen.
- **Read your writing out loud.** Writing also sounds different when the words are spoken, which is an important test of writing fluency. Use your speech as a guide to revise complicated words and passages: *If you wouldn't say it that way, don't write it that way.*
- **Have a peer read it.** Ask for specific changes you can make to upgrade the quality of your writing.
- **Keep an open mind.** Others will see things you cannot; try new ideas, even if they feel uncomfortable at first. You can toss

out ideas that don't work after you have given them a chance to expand your thinking.

While paragraph length is a judgment call, keeping paragraphs between four and eight sentences helps ensure your writing remains reader friendly. Once again, when papers are short, keep your paragraphs short. For a shorter paragraph, use three or four sentences to explain, expand, and support your topic sentence. When papers are long, give yourself more leeway with paragraph length.

Recap

While you cannot depend on a recipe to write a paragraph, you can rely on a few guidelines:

- By breaking your writing into manageable chunks, you make your ideas more accessible.
- By putting the topic sentence at the beginning of the paragraph and then building a topic string, you develop a cohesive paragraph.
- By applying principles of information flow, you can develop paragraphs that have a logical flow and are coherent.
- By applying a consistent viewpoint, you ensure that a paragraph is grammatically correct; and by using the third-person viewpoint, you meet academic expectations.

WRITING WORKSHOP

Editing Paragraphs

Instructions: Select a paper you have previously written. Identify two or three paragraphs to revise. As you edit and revise your writing, also analyze the kinds of changes you are making. Which principles are you applying to improve the quality and flow of your writing?

This assignment consists of the following parts: revising your original writing (two to three paragraphs), analyzing the changes you made, and creating a process message:

1. **For the revision,** use Microsoft Word's track changes feature.

    a. In the Review tab in your Word toolbar, click on Track Changes to record markup of the changes you are making.

    b. Save two copies of your revision: one with tracking on and one with tracking off.

2. **In the analysis,** discuss the changes you made and principles that you applied.

    a. Did you identify and revise any sentences longer than 25 words?

    b. Did you break each paragraph into eight or fewer sentences?

    c. Can you identify the topic sentence of each paragraph?

    d. Does each sentence in the paragraph develop the topic string?

    e. Did you cut empty or irrelevant information?

    f. Is each paragraph cohesive and coherent?

3. **For the process message,** discuss what you learned about editing sentences and paragraphs as well as any changes you are making in your writing.

    a. Attach two copies of your revision: one with tracking on and one with tracking off.

    b. So that you send only one attachment, place both copies in the same Word document.

References

APA. (2020). *Publication manual for the American Psychological Association* (7th ed.). https://doi.org/10.1037/0000165-000

Author Note: M. Ellis, BSN major at Indiana University Northwest, contributed to this chapter.

Designing Virtual Experiential Learning Opportunities

for Health Information Management Education

Linda Galocy

Indiana University

EDUC Y711: Readings in Instructional Technology

Dr. Thomas Brush

Fall 2020

[The following literature review was written by Linda Galocy for her class, Readings in Instructional Technology, EDUC Y711, in preparation for receiving her Ed.D. in Instructional Systems Technology at Indiana University.]

Abstract

This literature review explores experiential learning programs that have conducted virtual learning experiences, identifies emerging themes, and identifies areas for further research. Experiential learning is defined in the context of Health Information Management (HIM). Experiential learning is aligned with constructivist and experiential learning theories, and several instructional models aligned with these theories are presented. Two emerging themes for instructional design are skills development and community partnerships. Finally, the literature provides several challenges to virtual experiential learning, such as the identifying technological issues for students and testing instructional models in other settings due to small study sizes.

Keywords: experiential learning programs, health information management, virtual learning for undergraduates, instructional design models

Designing Virtual Experiential Learning Opportunities

for Health Information Management Education

Health Information Management (HIM) is a healthcare

discipline that combines business, science, and information

technology. HIM is the discipline that acquires and analyzes

patient data and protects medical information, regardless of its

format, that is essential to providing healthcare to patients and

to manage the business of healthcare (CAHIIM, 2018).

According to the Commission on Accreditation for

Health Informatics and Information Management Education

(CAHIIM), HIM students are required to complete "a

minimum of 40 hours of externally supervised activity prior

to graduation" (2019, p. 9). Thus, experiential learning,

as it fits into the HIM educational program, requires

externally supervised activity. However, the pandemic has

created challenges for an HIM educator's ability to arrange

experiential learning opportunities in a traditional, face-to-

face healthcare setting.

As an alternative, students can benefit from a virtual experience through participation in their future workplace reality: a virtual experience can help students further develop their soft skills, improve their self-confidence, and increase their professional network. Also, by interacting in diverse environments, students can draw upon and reinforce their academic knowledge. Virtual experiential learning can also provide students with greater external supervised activity options because geography will no longer be a factor (Ruggiero & Boehm, 2016).

With the sudden transition to remote learning in the spring and summer of 2020, the impact of virtual learnings was quickly realized. This literature review explores experiential learning programs that have conducted virtual learning experiences, identifying emerging themes and determining the gaps in research related to the design and development of courses. Unfortunately, there is a lack of literature in the Health Information field directed towards professional practice in virtual settings.

Defining Experiential Learning

CAHIIM (2019) defines experiential learning

as a professional practice experience that reinforces

didactic instruction to apply that knowledge at healthcare

organizations. This definition is also used to inform virtual

experiential learning as it relates to Health Information

Management education. The Association for Experiential

Education (n.d.) provides a more straightforward definition in

that this is a hands-on learning experience that then requires

a process of reflection. There are also different forms of

experiential learning, such as role-playing exercises, games,

field projects, case studies, or external activities.

As it applies to this literature review, the format of

experiential learning are external activities that are supervised

by a professional mentor. There is an added layer of difficulty

of how to apply hands-on learning virtually. A professional

practice experience needs to be designed so that a student is

paired with an HIM professional mentor to meet the external

supervision requirement. Activities must be a part of the

DESIGNING LEARNING OPPORTUNITIES   5

design to achieve higher level competencies, such as analysis,

evaluation, and synthesis. Assessments are meant to validate

the knowledge that students have learned in the classroom and

are effectively applied in the practice setting.

Work-integrated learning or WIL is commonly used

throughout the literature to describe experiential learning.

The *International Journal of Work-Integrated Learning*

(2020) defines WIL as creating a work-based experience to

integrate theory with a work practice intentionally. To do this

effectively, students, the university, and the workplace all

work together to create an authentic experience and provide

meaningful engagement in work-related tasks. This definition

encapsulates the focus of this paper. Accredited HIM

programs are required to provide students with relevant work-

based experiences. To change to virtual learning experiences

and what is described in this literature review, the clinical

coordinator is the educator, and the external supervisor is the

professional mentor.

Themes for Virtual Experiential Learning Opportunities

Two themes emerged from the literature and are identified as important to the scope of this review. These are essential considerations for a robust virtual experiential learning program. The first is the need to develop skills for the remote workforce, and this skill development includes the instructor, student, and mentor. The second is the establishment of and maintenance of strong community partnerships.

Instructional Models

Throughout a review of the literature, instructional models aligned with the constructivist learning theory and experiential learning theory are reviewed. The instructional models discussed are virtual attachment theory, service-learning theory, and boundary theory. Research by Channell and Anderson (2010) is a case study following eight principles of good practice for experiential learning as adapted from the National Society for Experiential Education.

While not an instructional model, the design of the experience and discussion that follows validates that a virtual internship can provide a similar educational experience when compared to the traditional face-to-face experience.

Experiential Learning Theory. Culminating in over one hundred years of contributions by several scholars, experiential learning theory was developed by William James, John Dewey, Kurt Lewin, Jean Piaget, Lev Vygotsky, Carl Jung, Mary Parker Follett, Carl Rogers, and Paulo Friere (Kolb & Kolb, 2017). The framework of this theory is presented as a cycle. The student is involved in a concrete experience that they then reflect on. There is a point in the cycle where abstract conceptualization occurs, which is when the student can grasp or fully realize the value of their experience, and finally, culminating in active experimentation. Achieving the active experimentation phase is the goal for all students to reach. This phase is the point at which students can truly apply what they learned. It is important to include the facilitator or educator and the mentor or external supervisor throughout this entire cycle. At the center of the experience is the student, with the educator and mentor guiding the student through each of the four phases of the cycle. The authors found that a unique relationship is established between the student, teacher, and mentor and that everyone was increasing their knowledge, adding perspective, questioning differences, and challenging each other. According to Kolb and Kolb (2017), this is the magic of experiential learning.

Constructivist Learning Theory. This student-centered approach suggests learning occurs best through authentic experiences. Dewey and Vygotsky are the most notable early constructivists, and one can see how their work has led to the experiential learning theory. An impact that Dewey had towards experiential learning theory is the point in the cycle of reflection. He argued that it is important to stop and reflect and learn in a typical learning experience. This reflection helps to create meaning from the experience

DESIGNING LEARNING OPPORTUNITIES   9

and can be used for a future experience (Kolb & Kolb, 2017). The importance of reflection is discussed as it relates to experiential learning. Reflection is the point at which students realize what they have learned.

Faucette and Nugent (2015) discuss a few assumptions to constructivist learning theory. The first assumption is that the student-centered learning approach includes self-directed learning, where the learner can discover new skills within themselves. Another assumption is that given opportunities to discuss and reflect with peers while going through their experiences; new knowledge is constructed. The educator's role in this process is to ensure that all students realize this new knowledge.

Virtual Attachment Theory. This learning theory applies to adults within a community of inquiry framework (CoI). As students are introduced to mentors in the professional settings to which they are assigned, and as a relationship is developed, secure attachments between learner and mentor will be achieved. The three fundamental principles of virtual attachment theory are communication,

guidance, and work quality. Research by Ruggeiro and

Boehm (2016) looked at three groups of interns, analyzed

their communication patterns, work quality, and three types

of relationships developed as a part of their experience: intern

and client, intern and mentor, and mentor to client.

The pattern they discovered was that if interns had a

positive relationship with their mentors, and the mentors had

good relationships with their clients, the interns demonstrated

more independence, a more precise and consistent

communication style, and a greater willingness to be guided

by their mentor. This theory makes sense that if a healthy

relationship is established, the more confidence the student

will have in their work quality. However, as noted by the

authors, this study's limitations were that this theory requires

further research to determine if that impact and quality of

work will hold.

DESIGNING LEARNING OPPORTUNITIES   11

Service-Learning. An approach to learning that suggests students learn best by applying their knowledge while engaged with others in the workforce (Pike, 2017), service-learning includes preparation, completion of the activity, and guided reflection during and after the experience. Projects are mutually beneficial, and students are applying their didactic knowledge to a real-world project.

Boundary Theory. As discussed by Bowen (2020), boundary theory is used as the foci to describe students' challenges and how to overcome them in a remote WIL environment. Bowen conducted a literature review examining the complexities of remote working while focusing on students' need to become self-directed learners as the workforce moved to online and remote work. Boundary theory explains that individuals learn to manage the boundaries between work and personal life (Bulger et al., 2007). Using boundary theory as a focus for online experiential learning design, instructors and mentors can help students define and develop their physical and temporal

boundaries to help the student develop a professional mindset

for the remote workplace. A student's professionalism must

consider twenty-first century skills, and an instructor or

mentor can only facilitate a student's development.

Eight Principles of Good Practice

The National Society for Experiential Education

(2013) developed a framework titled "Eight Principles of

Good Practice for All Experiential Learning Activities."

The eight principles provide a foundation for educators for

creating effective experiential education opportunities. These

principles were used to design a virtual experiential learning

opportunity for music business interns. The eight principles

are as follows:

1. **intention:** Expected outcomes and goals and objectives
   for projects are written.

2. **preparedness and planning:** Clear expectations, start,
   and end dates are understood by all parties.

DESIGNING LEARNING OPPORTUNITIES 13

3. **authenticity:** There must be real-world experiences.

4. **reflection:** The intern must be allowed to reflect on what they have learned. The mentor should reflect on the work attempted by the student.

5. **orientation and training:** The intern should be provided with an orientation experience like that of a new employee and expectations of how projects are typically completed. The culture of an organization and its structure is essential for the student to understand.

6. **monitoring and continuous improvement:** The intern should receive consistent feedback, crucial to their learning process.

7. **assessment and evaluation:** The mentor is responsible for assessing skills and providing feedback to the student.

8. **acknowledgment:** The mentor, student, and educator should acknowledge all the accomplishments achieved during the experience.

DESIGNING LEARNING OPPORTUNITIES   14

The relevant importance of these eight principles

is that a well-designed remote learning experience should

expand the opportunities in which students can engage

with the use of technology, a requirement for the remote

workforce. These eight principles also demonstrate many

similarities to experiential learning theory.

Skill Development for Educators, Students, and Mentors

There are many skills that research has identified as

essential to develop and improve upon for educators, students,

and professional mentors to ensure effective experiential

learning outcomes. The first is the use of technology. The

technology used as a learner can be different than what is

used in the workforce. Working in virtual teams, working

collaboratively, and developing leadership skills is important

as students transition into the workforce. The preparation of

the educator and professional mentor also cannot be ignored.

A traditional experiential learning opportunity requires

a different skill set than what educators and mentors are

used to. All individuals involved in the virtual experiential learning acquired more sophisticated organizational skills and found areas to improve their communication skills. The development of many of these skills, particularly for the student in an undergraduate program, is essential to ensure that they are prepared for the workforce (Loucks & Ozogul, 2020).

Technological Skills. A remote workforce is reliant on technology. A well-designed learning experience should provide the student with opportunities to work on projects, communicate with mentors, and learn the profession using technology that is most current in the workplace (Channell & Anderson, 2010). Students utilize different technology platforms but often do not know how to work collaboratively in a work environment (Long & Meglich, 2013). The technology they know has been used to meet student learning outcomes in the classroom setting. The technology used in the workplace accomplishes much more than just meeting learning outcomes.

DESIGNING LEARNING OPPORTUNITIES   16

For example, students in a Health Information

Management program can access various electronic systems

that are utilized in an actual healthcare organization.

They may also participate in a class session via a video-

conferencing platform, use email and discussion boards.

In a real healthcare organization, and as a part of a virtual

learning experience, the student can access similar electronic

platforms but work with live patient data and systems that are

integrated. The student can also participate in meetings either

live or through video-conferencing platforms, learn how to

manage projects through productivity management software,

using technology to work collaboratively.

This authentic, real-world experience will help the

student apply knowledge learned in the classroom (Faucette

& Nugent, 2015) and attain higher-level thinking skills as

defined by the Taxonomy of Educational Objectives (Bloom,

1984) that the CAHIIM requires. It is assumed that a student

has learned to prioritize and organize according to class

DESIGNING LEARNING OPPORTUNITIES   17

schedules, but this is not the same as the world of work,

especially in healthcare.

     Organizational Skills. Educator skill sets that need

improvement for a virtual experience are organizational

skills and improved support for learners. Educators need to

be flexible, understand individual students' learning needs,

and be open to new technologies (Faucette & Nugent,

2015). Other skills required of educators indicated the need

for continued interaction between all students completing

their virtual experiences as this helps to motivate students.

There is also a need for the instructor to provide specific and

focused feedback on deliverables the student is preparing for

the mentor and guide the student to reflect on their learning

experience actively.

     If an HIM educator is accustomed to online teaching,

and their students are used to online learning, communication

may need to be altered from prior expectations. In other

words, the educator may want to be more accessible to their

students to provide more instant help, feedback, and guidance

to students. For example, suppose an online instructor has

used email or asynchronous discussion boards to manage

student communication in other online courses, with virtual

experiences. In that case, a shift to instant messaging, phone

calls, texting, or other instant communication methods should

be considered.

Areas for Further Research

The literature provided several challenges to virtual

experiential learning, such as the lack of formal engagement

of students to mentors, pushback by individuals that may

not be amenable to changing an experience to a virtual

opportunity, and instructors concerned with creating online

experiences authentically. These challenges are valid, and

further research needs to be done to demonstrate how the

challenges can be overcome. An issue that fell outside the

parameters of this literature review was the consideration of

technology and privacy and security issues, particularly for

DESIGNING LEARNING OPPORTUNITIES   19

healthcare programs. Finally, the size of the studies is very

small, so certainly more comparison studies can be performed

to test the transferability and results of the instructional

models to other programs.

One challenge identified in the literature was the lack

of students' informal engagement with other students, their

instructors, and the organization. Salter et al. (2020) made

the point that this lack of engagement may have the potential

to lack some creativity that tends to come when at a physical

location. Following experiential learning theory as a guide,

the instructor could reinforce what the student has learned

by reviewing the learning outcomes, highlight what they did

accomplish, and review the specific feedback provided by

their peers, mentor, and instructor. These steps should give

assurances that they did learn and missing out on informal

conversations would not have changed the outcome.

The literature provides examples of using real-world

tasks in classroom learning environments, but few studies

show how instructors can make online learning experiences authentic. Instructors are challenged with the management and teaching of online courses. Specifically, high enrollment courses preclude instructors from providing the feedback and attention that students desire. Loucks and Ozogul (2020) used the cascading strategy to teach virtual leadership skills in their descriptive case study. They indicated that high enrollment courses are challenging for an instructor, specifically to evaluate and provide feedback to students. The authors suggested that a way to overcome this would be to incorporate coaching strategies when teaching leadership skills. Providing students with the opportunity to lead teams throughout the course, and having the instructor provide feedback to each team lead throughout the semester would reduce the number of assessments needing to be done at one time.

The research provided instructional models aligned with cognitive and experiential learning theories to design virtual learning experiences. Still, the studies were small, therefore difficult to determine if the results of those studies

could be transferred to other settings. Salter et al. (2020) had

to quickly change to remote experiential learning for nursing

students. They were the clinical placement coordinators and

only presented four case studies limiting the conclusions

they provided. Faucette and Nugent (2015), in their research

of K–12 preservice learning teachers undergoing their own

virtual internship experiences, indicated that their small

sample size of 8 students prevented generalization of results

to other sites and populations.

Ruggiero and Boehm (2016) designed a virtual

internship program applying virtual attachment theory. Their

study was also limited by small numbers of students and

client selection. Ruggiero and Boehm (2016) discussed that

virtual attachment theory needed further testing to identify the

framework's impact on the relationship to the work quality of

program development.

Finally, there is a lack of literature in the Health Information field directed towards professional practice in virtual settings.

Conclusion

The literature review provided a wide variety of case studies and applications for virtual experiential learning opportunities. As the workforce, in general, has found it necessary to adapt and utilize technology to meet the goals of a company in new ways, education must adapt and teach students to graduate in this type of work environment successfully. Higher education's importance in creating or strengthening their relationships to the community is essential in helping students learn to adapt or learn new skills for a future remote work setting. Research that includes community partnerships and effectively links educational theory to virtual experiential learning will further create a more robust design and even more positive student outcomes.

References

Bowen, T. (2020). Work-integrated learning placements and

remote working: Experiential learning online. *Inter-

national Journal of Work-Integrated Learning, 21*(4),

377–386.

Bloom, B. (Ed.). (1984). *The taxonomy of educational objec-

tives.* Addison Wesley.

Bulger, C. A., Matthews, R. A., & Hoffman, M. E. (2007).

Work and Personal Life Boundary Management:

Boundary Strength, Work/Personal Life Balance, and

the Segmentation-Integration Continuum. *Journal of

Occupational Health Psychology, 12*(4), 365–375.

https://doi.org/10.1037/1076-8998.12.4.365

Channell, T. L., & Anderson, D. M. (2010). Creating Virtual

Internships in the Music Business. *MEIEA Journal:

Journal of the Music & Entertainment Industry Edu-

cators Association, 10*(1), 173–185.

Commission on Accreditation for Health Informatics and

    Information Management. (2019). *2018 Accreditation*

    Standards Health Information Management Bac-

    calaureate Degree. Retrieved November 10, 2020,

    from https://www.cahiim.org/docs/default-source/

    accreditation/health-information-management/him-

    standards/4-3-1-2018-standards-him-baccalaureate.

    pdf?sfvrsn=3aec83d2_8

Faucette, N., & Nugent, P. (2015). Impacts of a redesigned

    virtual internship program on preservice teachers'

    skills and attitudes. *International Journal of*

    E-Learning & Distance Education, 30(2), 1–15.

Global Workplace Analytics. (2020). *Telecommuting*

    trend data. https://globalworkplace analytics.com/

    telecommuting-statistics

International Journal of Work-Integrated Learning. (n.d.).

    Home. https://www.ijwil.org/

DESIGNING LEARNING OPPORTUNITIES   25

Kolb, A. Y., & Kolb, D. A. (2017). Experiential learning

    theory as a guide for experiential educators in higher

    education. *ELTHE: A Journal for Engaged Educators,*

    1(1), 7–45. Retrieved from https://nsuworks.nova.edu/

    elthe/vol1/iss1/7

Long, L. K., & Meglich, P. A. (2013). Preparing students to

    collaborate in the virtual work world. *Higher Edu-*

    cation, Skills and Work-Based Learning, 3(1), 6–16.

    https://doi.org/10.1108/20423891311294948

Loucks, S., & Ozogul, G. (2020). Preparing business stu-

    dents for a distributed workforce and global business

    environment: Gaining virtual leadership skills in an

    authentic context. *TechTrends, 64*(4), 655–665. https://

    doi.org/10.1007/s11528-020-00513-4

National Society for Experiential Education. (2011). *Eight*

    principles of good practice for all experiential learn-

    ing activities. https://www.nsee.org/8-principles

Ruggiero, D., & Boehm, J. (2016). Design and develop-

    ment of a learning design virtual internship program.

International Review of Research in Open and Distance Learning, 17(4), 105–120. https://doi. org/10.19173/irrodl.v17i4.2385

Salter, C., Oates, R. K., Swanson, C., & Bourke, L. (2020). Working remotely: Innovative allied health placements in response to COVID-19. *International Journal of Work-Integrated Learning, 21*(5), 587–600.

U.S. Department of Health & Human Services. (2020). *Notification of enforcement discretion for telehealth.* https:// www.hhs.gov/hipaa/for-professionals/special-topics/ emergency-preparedness/notification-enforcement- discretion-telehealth/index.html

What is ee? (n.d.). Association for Experiential Education. Retrieved December 13, 2020, from https://www.aee. org/what-is-ee

Wiley Education Services. (2020). *4 types of undergraduate students* [Infographic]. Edservices. wiley.com. https://edservices.wiley.com/

four-types-of-undergraduate-students/?utm_

source=WatsonMailing&utm_medium=email&utm_

campaign=201604-WES-CORP-Misc-UndergradSur-

vey-20201202%20(1)&utm_content=&spMailingID

=32829002&sp UserID=MzczMzU4NDg3N-

TYyS0&spJobID=1843090827&sp

PART III

Editing Your Paper

9

COMMA RULES, NOT PAUSES

For APA style (and all academic and professional writing), using commas correctly is fundamental. Since comma usage is primarily determined by sentence structure, APA style is not unique in the rules it requires writers to apply.

If you are unsure of how to use commas correctly, take time to review the comma rules in this chapter. For example, many writers use commas to "pause" or to "take a breath." If you use commas as pauses, you are likely to be making serious errors in your writing, possibly unknowingly.

The pause approach turns punctuating into a guessing game, resulting in run-on sentences and fragments. These types of errors cause writers to lose credibility. Start this chapter with a fresh way of thinking. Take the time to review the rules thoroughly, and when you use a comma know the rule that applies.

In general, when in doubt about comma use, leave out the comma. When you are uncertain, research to see if a rule applies. And when all else fails, rewrite the sentence in a way you know is correct. Though comma rules vary slightly from source to source, the comma rules presented in this chapter are consistent with other sources, including APA guidelines.

When you complete this chapter, you will be able to

- apply 12 basic comma rules to your writing,

- use commas correctly for parenthetical in-text citations, and
- use commas correctly when setting off statistics.

In-Text Citations and Statistics

Before reviewing the 12 basic comma rules that pertain to all types of writing, let's first take a look at two types of comma usage that occur frequently in APA style.

Parenthetical Citations

For in-text citations, use a comma to separate each part of a parenthetical citation. Parenthetical citations can include authors' names, the year of publication, and page numbers.

> **incorrect:** Critical decisions are made at each stage of the process. (Davidson 1998)

> **correct:** Critical decisions are made at each stage of the process (Davidson, 1998).

> **incorrect:** In most countries studied, "processed foods provide only about half of people's sodium intake." (Davidson 1998, page 221)

> **correct:** In most countries studied, "processed foods provide only about half of people's sodium intake" (Davidson, 1998, p. 221).

In each of the corrected examples, the period is placed on the outside of the parenthetical citation. This comma usage is related to Rule 6: Parentheticals (see page 193–194).

Statistics

Use commas and semicolons to set off statistics within parentheses. This rule helps writers reduce the use of parentheses and brackets for complicated constructions.

> The pilot studies included similar profiles (Adams: M = 7, F = 7; Rogers: M = 9, F = 8).

In this example, a semicolon was used to separate major elements; this usage is similar to Rule 3: Semicolon Because of Comma in Chapter 10 (see pages 206–207).

Punctuation and Purpose

In narrative writing, the purpose of punctuation is to break language into grammatical units, dividing groups of words into sentences and clauses. Punctuation is the glue that holds language together. To place commas in context, we review some grammar basics in this section.

For most sentences the subject precedes the verb, and the verb determines the subject. Throughout this chapter, examples are displayed to highlight the structure of the sentence; the subject is underlined once, and the verb is underlined twice.

Subject – verb – object.

An *independent clause* contains a subject and verb and can stand on its own; an independent clause is a complete sentence. When independent clauses are joined without sufficient punctuation, the result is a *run-on sentence.* To correct a run-on sentence, you can do the following:

- If a coordinating conjunction (e.g., "and," "but," or "or") connects the clauses, place a comma before it. See Rule 2: Conjunction (CONJ; page 190).
- Separate the clauses with a semicolon. See Rule 1: Semicolon with No Conjunction (NC; page 205).

A *dependent clause* has a subject and verb but cannot stand alone. When a dependent clause is punctuated as a sentence, the result is a *fragment.* To turn a dependent clause into a complete sentence, you can do the following:

- Combine the dependent clause with a sentence that precedes or follows it.
- Remove the subordinating conjunction at the beginning of the clause. Common subordinating conjunctions are "if," "after," "before," "because," "since," "although," and so on. See Review

Point: Conjunctions as Signals (page 191) and Rule 4: Introductory (INTRO; pages 191–192).

As you review comma and semicolon rules, pay attention to sentence structure; if you have challenges with run-ons and fragments read sentences out loud. By learning how to punctuate correctly, you learn structure, which is the foundation of developing sound editing skills. Good writing is a function of good editing—no one writes perfectly, and everyone can produce good writing through effective editing.

Rule 1: The Sentence Core Rules (SCR)

Do not separate a subject and verb with only one comma. Though this rule does not indicate where you need to place a comma, it keeps you from making serious errors. In the following example, the subject of each sentence is underlined once, and the verb is underlined twice.

incorrect: The <u>foundation</u>, <u>accepted</u> my grant proposal.

correct: The <u>foundation</u> <u>accepted</u> my grant proposal.

Whenever you put one comma between a subject and verb, take out the comma or check to see if you need to add a second comma. If you write run-on sentences, the next rule will assist you significantly in learning how correct those types of errors.

> ### REVIEW POINT
>
> To identify the sentence core, identify the verb first and then the subject, which precedes the verb in statements. At times, a sentence will have an *understood* or *implied subject*.
>
> (<u>You</u>) Give your information to Lucile.
>
> (<u>I</u>) Thank you for your help.
>
> When it seems difficult to identify the subject that precedes a verb, ask yourself if the subject could be an implied subject, such as "you understood" (You) or "I understood" (I).

Rule 2: Conjunction (CONJ)

Put a comma before a *coordinating conjunction* (e.g., "and," "but," "or," "for," "nor," "so," and "yet") when it connects two independent clauses. The two most common coordinating conjunctions are "and" and "but." Place a comma before a coordinating conjunction when an independent clause precedes it and follows it.

> **incorrect:** The project was approved but we cannot start until next month.

> **correct:** The project was approved, but we cannot start until next month.

The previous incorrect example is a *run-on sentence*: two or more sentences coming together without sufficient punctuation.

Though some writers automatically put a comma before "and," a comma is not always needed. Use a comma in a compound sentence.

> **incorrect:** Bob worked on the proposal and he sent it to my supervisor.

> **correct:** Bob worked on the proposal, and he sent it to my supervisor.

> **compound sentence:** Bob worked … , and he sent …

Do not, however, use a comma for a compound verb with the same subject.

> **incorrect:** Bob worked on the proposal, and sent it to my supervisor.

> **correct:** Bob worked on the proposal and sent it to my supervisor.

> **compound verb with the same subject:** Bob worked … and sent …

Rule 3: Series (SER)

Put a comma between items in a series. A series consists of three or more items; place a comma between each item.

> **incorrect:** The statistician tallied the mean, median and average.

> **correct:** The statistician tallied the mean, median, and average.

The comma preceding "and" is referred to as an *Oxford comma*; while some sources state the Oxford comma is optional, APA style requires the Oxford comma. In fact, using the Oxford comma increases clarity.

A common mistake is placing a comma before "and" when it connects only two items.

incorrect: The assistant provided a series of examples, and a good recap of the meeting.

correct: The assistant provided a series of examples and a good recap of the meeting.

The error of placing a comma in a list with only two items often occurs when the items are long phrases, as in the previous example above.

REVIEW POINT

Conjunctions as Signals

Following are the three types of conjunctions that play a role in punctuation, along with a few examples of each:

- **coordinating conjunctions:** and, but, or, nor, for, so, yet
- **subordinating conjunctions:** if, after, while, when, as, although, because, as soon as
- **adverbial conjunctions:** however, therefore, thus, for example, in conclusion

Conjunctions also play a role in creating a reader-friendly writing style because they cue the reader to the meaning you are conveying.

Rule 4: Introductory (INTRO)

Put a comma after a word, phrase, or dependent clause that introduces an independent clause. Since this rule is a bit complicated, the following list offers a review of each of the various parts:

- **word:** In general, "word" refers to an adverbial conjunction, such as "therefore," "however," and "consequently," among others.

  However, I was not able to attend the conference.

  Therefore, we will convene the meeting in Boston.

- **phrase:** in general, "phrase" refers to a prepositional phrase, a gerund phrase, or an infinitive phrase.

  During that time, they spoke about the plan in detail.

  Finishing my study early, I started the article sooner than expected.

  To arrive earlier, Michael rearranged his entire schedule.

- **dependent clause:** a dependent clause begins with a subordinating conjunction, such as "since," "because," "although," "while," "if," and so on.

  Although my calendar is full, we can meet this Friday.

  Before you arrive at my office, (you) call my assistant.

  Until I am available, you can work in an extra office.

Placing a comma after a subordinating conjunction is a common mistake.

> **incorrect:** *Although*, the information is timely, we cannot use it.

> **correct:** *Although* the information is timely, we cannot use it.

Do not place the comma after the subordinating conjunction; place the comma after the dependent clause.

Rule 5: Nonrestrictive (NR)

Use commas to set off explanations that are nonessential to the meaning of the sentence. To apply this rule correctly, review the difference between *restrictive* and *nonrestrictive information*. Restrictive information is essential, while nonrestrictive information is not essential.

Nonrestrictive elements, which often come in the form of "who" or "which" clauses, should be set off with commas. The two following examples illustrate this rule ("who" clauses are italicized); the first illustrates a nonrestrictive appositive and the second, a restrictive appositive.

Dr. Neal Barnard, *who is a prestigious author*, will be the keynote speaker.

The doctor *who is a prestigious author* will be the keynote speaker.

In the first example, you would still know who the keynote speaker would be if the "who" clause were removed. However, in the second example, the meaning of the sentence would be unclear if the "who" clause were removed.

The doctor will be the keynote speaker.

In the previous example, it is unclear which doctor will be the keynote speaker. In fact, all commas that come in sets imply that the information set off by the commas can be removed, so here is another reminder of how to use commas with *essential* and *nonessential information*:

- **Essential information** is restrictive and *should* not *be set off with commas.*
- **Nonessential information** is nonrestrictive and *can be set off with commas.*

Rule 6: Parenthetical (PAR)

Use commas to set off a word or expression that interrupts the flow of a sentence. This rule applies to adverbial conjunctions or other short phrases interjected into a sentence.

Parenthetical expressions should be set off with commas. They are nonessential and can be removed, leaving the sentence complete and clear in meaning.

Mr. Connors, *however*, arrived after the opening ceremony.

You can, *therefore*, place your order after 5 p.m. today.

The project, *in my opinion*, needs improvement.

A common mistake occurs when a writer uses a semicolon in place of one of the commas.

incorrect: Ms. Philippe; in fact, approved the request last week.

correct: Ms. Philippe, in fact, approved the request last week.

When a semicolon precedes an adverbial conjunction, two sentences are generally involved; the adverbial conjunction functions as a bridge or a transition rather than an interrupter. See Chapter 10 for more information.

Another common mistake occurs when a writer uses only one comma rather than a set of commas.

incorrect: Our outreach team, therefore will assist you at your convenience.

correct: Our outreach team, therefore, will assist you at your convenience.

incorrect: Mr. Jones, however will plan this year's event.

correct: Mr. Jones, however, will plan this year's event.

To improve the flow of the sentence, bring the adverbial conjunction to the beginning of the sentence.

However, Mr. Jones will plan this year's event.

Also, comments such as "I believe" or "I think" are not adverbial conjunctions, and it is generally best to edit them out of your writing.

with adverbial conjunction: *I think* the answer will become clear as we move forward.

without adverbial conjunction: The answer will become clear as we move forward.

Can you see how these changes make a sentence flow more effectively?

Rule 7: Direct Address (DA)

Use commas to set off the name or title of a person addressed directly. Often, the name of the person being addressed directly appears at the beginning of the sentence; however, the person's name can also appear in the middle or at the end of the sentence, as in the following example.

Charles, you arrange the details for the upcoming conference in Louisville.

I invited the entire department to the holiday potluck, *Eileen.*

Your instructions, *Professor*, were clear and to the point.

In each of these examples, notice that the name of the person being addressed is not the subject of the sentence. In sentences that contain a direct address, the subject is often implied.

(I) Thank you, *Dr. Parsons*, for speaking on my behalf.

(You) Feel free to call my office at your convenience, *Oscar.*

Rule 8: Appositive (AP)

Use commas to set off the restatement of a noun or pronoun. With an appositive, an equivalency exists between the noun and its descriptor. In the following examples, the appositives are shown in italics.

Kelley, *my colleague from New York*, acquired the information from a reliable source.

Mr. Ginther, *professor emeritus*, assisted with the statistical analysis.

When an appositive occurs in the middle of a sentence, using only one comma not only creates a mistake but also changes the meaning of the sentence. Notice how the following sentences differ in meaning.

incorrect: Shadrack, my former department chair insisted on the due date.

correct: Shadrack, my former department chair, insisted on the due date.

This rule applies to appositives that are not restrictive, but some appositives are restrictive. In the following example, it is assumed the writer has more than one colleague.

restrictive AP: My colleague Charles will attend the July workshop.

If "Charles" were removed from the sentence, it would be unclear which colleague would be attending the workshop. Thus, for a *restrictive appositive*, omit the commas.

Rule 9: Addresses and Dates (AD)

Use commas to set off the parts of addresses and dates. The term "set off" means commas are placed on both sides of the part of the address or date to show separation. For example, notice how commas surround "Illinois" and "California" as well as "August 15."

Chicago, Illinois, is the best city to host the conference.

Sally has resided in San Francisco, California, since the hospital opened.

On Friday, August 15, our nurses celebrated the results of the accrediting commission's report.

Does it surprise you to learn that a comma is required after a state name? If so, you are not alone; the following mistake is common.

incorrect: Dallas, Texas is hosting this year's annual meeting.

correct: Dallas, Texas, is hosting this year's annual meeting.

The same is true for dates; the second comma in the set is often left off incorrectly.

incorrect: Professor Barnes recorded September 10, 2021 as the date the project began.

correct: Professor Barnes recorded September 10, 2021, as the date the project began.

Another type of error occurs when a writer puts a comma between the month and the day.

incorrect: October, 21, 2019 was the date on the application.

correct: October 21, 2019, was the date on the application.

Never put a comma between the month and the day, as shown in the previous incorrect example.

Rule 10: Word Omitted (WO)

Use a comma in place of a word or words that play a structural role in a sentence. This type of comma occurs infrequently. Most of the time, the word omitted is either "that" or "and."

original: The idea is *that* changing the course name will attract more participants.

WO: The idea is, changing the course name will attract more participants.

original: Dr. Haggen presented a long *and* boring PowerPoint at the conference.

WO: Dr. Haggen presented a long, boring PowerPoint at the conference.

Rule 11: Direct Quotation (DQ)

Use commas to set off a direct quotation within a sentence. A direct quotation is a person's exact words. In comparison, an indirect quotation does not give a speaker's exact words and should not be set off with commas. An exception to this rule relates to short quotations: a short quotation built into the flow of a sentence does not need to be set off with commas.

The attendant shouted "Stop!" as they entered the closed building.

My manager advised me "This too shall end" as we discussed the changes.

When my coach said "Give this your best," I felt motivated.

With direct quotations, whether you are setting off short quotations with commas or blending them with the flow of the sentence, capitalize the first word of the quotation. Since using punctuation with quotation marks can be confusing, apply the following closed punctuation guidelines:

- Place commas and periods on the inside of quotation marks.
- Place semicolons and colons on the outside of quotation marks.
- Place exclamation marks and question marks based on meaning; these marks can go on the inside or outside of quotation marks.

Regardless of where the punctuation mark is placed, never double punctuate at the end of a sentence.

incorrect: The message was marked urgent, "Arrive promptly at 10 a.m.!".

correct: The message was marked urgent, "Arrive promptly at 10 a.m.!"

Rule 12: Contrasting Expression or Afterthought (CEA)

Use a comma to separate a *contrasting expression* or *afterthought* from the main clause. A contrasting expression or afterthought adds an interesting twist to writing style. The expression following a CEA comma grabs the reader's attention.

Go ahead and complete the survey, if you have time.

The information will enhance the project, not detract from it.

Omitting the CEA comma is not a serious error; however, using the CEA comma makes your comments stand out and gives your writing a conversational flow.

Recap

Have you stopped placing commas on the basis of pauses? If so, the quality of your writing along with your confidence will improve each time you use commas consciously and correctly.

WRITING WORKSHOP

Part 1: Editing a Cover Letter

Instructions: Edit the draft cover letter, keeping the following in mind:

- Add paragraph breaks and commas, as needed.
- Feel free to tailor this exercise to your own job search by "filling in the brackets."
- Format your letter as a professional business letter by adding the following details: a dateline, an inside address, a salutation, and a closing.

As a recent graduate of ["X" College] I would like to be considered an applicant for the position in ["X"]. In my previous work experience I learned valuable professional skills such as ["X" and "X"]. I have also been commended for being ["X"] and ["X"]. Whether working on academic or professional projects I apply critical thinking and research skills which support core strengths needed as a ["X"]. I look forward to speaking with you on how my skills will benefit your organization. Thank you for your consideration. Please contact me via email at [yourname@bc.edu] or by phone at (555) 555-1234 to arrange for a convenient meeting time. Sincerely,

Part 2: Process Message

Instructions: Write your professor a *process message* discussing what you learned in this chapter. Also update your professor on any current assignments or progress you are making in class. *What are you learning? How are you applying it?*

COMMA RULES

1. **The Sentence Core Rules (SCR)**

   Do not separate a subject and verb with only one comma.

2. **Conjunction (CONJ)**

   Use a comma to separate two independent clauses when they are joined by a coordinating conjunction.

3. **Series (SER)**

   Use a comma to separate three or more items in a series.

4. **Introductory (INTRO)**

   Place a comma after a word, phrase, or dependent clause that introduces an independent clause.

5. **Nonrestrictive (NR)**

   Use commas to set off nonessential (nonrestrictive) words and phrases.

6. **Parenthetical (PAR)**

   Use commas to set off a word or expression that interrupts the flow of a sentence. For in-text citations, use a comma to separate each part of a parenthetical citation.

7. **Direct Address (DA)**

   Use commas to set off the name or title of a person addressed directly.

8. **Appositive (AP)**

   Use commas to set off the restatement of a noun or pronoun.

9. **Addresses and Dates (AD)**

   Use commas to set off the parts of addresses and dates.

10. **Word Omitted (WO)**

    Use a comma for the omission of a word or words that play a structural role in a sentence.

11. **Direct Quotation (DQ)**

    Use commas to set off direct quotations within a sentence.

12. **Contrasting Expression or Afterthought (CEA)**

    Use a comma to separate a contrasting expression or afterthought.

KEY TO EXERCISE

Cover Letter

August 3, 2023

Pat Dunkirk, Hiring Manager
XYZ Company
1200 North Michigan Avenue
Chicago, IL 60611

Dear Pat Dunkirk:

As a recent graduate of Best College, I would like to be considered an applicant for the position in nursing.

In my previous work experience, I learned valuable professional skills, such as effective communication and strong leadership abilities. I have also been commended for being detailed-oriented and a collaborative team player. Whether working on academic or professional projects, I apply critical thinking and research skills, which support core strengths needed as a nurse.

I look forward to speaking with you about how my skills will benefit your organization. Please contact me at [your contact information] or at [555-555-1234] to arrange for a convenient time to meet. My résumé is enclosed.

Sincerely,

Andy Smith
Enclosure: Résumé

10

SEMICOLONS, COLONS, AND DASHES

D o you avoid using semicolons because you are unsure of how to use them? What about colons and dashes? Take a bit of time to learn how to use these marks; they will enhance your writing by giving you choices and adding energy to your message. But more importantly, for APA style and academic writing, using these marks is not an option but rather, at times, a necessity:

- In those instances when you need a semicolon or colon but do not use one, you may end up with a run-on sentence.
- When you display a numerical, page, or date range, use a dash, not a hyphen.

In addition, punctuation speaks to your reader in subtle yet powerful ways:

- The semicolon draws connections for readers, showing relationships.
- The colon alerts readers to information that is being illustrated, placing stress on it.
- The dash highlights information, making it stand out.

Practice using the semicolon, colon, and dash until you feel comfortable using them. Then use them confidently but sparingly.

When you complete this chapter, you will

- be able to apply semicolons, colons, and dashes correctly in your writing,
- understand the roles of coordinating, subordinating, and adverbial conjunctions in the use of semicolons, and
- be able to revise fragments and run-ons into complete sentences.

The Semicolon

If you do not use semicolons, you are likely to put a comma where a semicolon belongs, creating a serious grammatical error. While semicolons are not similar to commas, they are similar to periods; semicolons, like periods, create major breaks in structure:

- A semicolon is a full stop that is not terminal.
- A period is a full stop that is terminal.

In other words, a period brings the sentence to an end, but a semicolon does not. Most of the time, the following general rule for using semicolons works: A semicolon can be used in place of a period. Therefore, when using a period would be incorrect, you probably should not use a semicolon either. This part of the chapter discusses three semicolon rules:

- semicolon no conjunction (NC)
- semicolon transition (TR)
- semicolon because of commas (BC)

As you learn the semicolon rules, stretch your skills and experiment using semicolons in your own writing. The semicolon communicates to readers that ideas are close in meaning. Semicolons add variety and keep writing from getting choppy when sentences are short.

Conjunctions

Conjunctions play a major role in comma and semicolon use. Here is a brief review of the three types of conjunctions:

- **Coordinating conjunctions** connect equal grammatical parts.

  examples: and, but, or, for, nor, so, and yet

- **Subordinating conjunctions** introduce dependent clauses and phrases.

  examples: after, while, because, although, before, though, if, as, and as soon as

- **Adverbial conjunctions** introduce or interrupt independent clauses.

  examples: however, therefore, for example, consequently, as a result, though, thus, and fortunately

Be cautious when a conjunction appears in the middle of a sentence, as it may signal the use of a semicolon (see Rule 2: Semicolon Transition and Rule 3: Semicolon Because of Commas).

Rule 1: Semicolon No Conjunction (NC)

Use a semicolon to separate two independent clauses that are joined without a conjunction. This semicolon is sometimes referred to as *semicolon in place of a period.* In fact, you can tell that you are using a semicolon correctly if you can substitute a period for it. Often a semicolon is used when one or both statements are short and related in meaning; the semicolon helps the reader infer the connection between the ideas.

comma conjunction: Simmons wrote the article, *but* he did not receive credit for it. (CONJ)

semicolon no conjunction: Simmons wrote the article; he did not receive credit for it. (NC)

period: Simmons wrote the article. He did not receive credit for it.

Do you hear how choppy the writing sounds in the example that uses a period? To avoid writing short, choppy sentences, use a semicolon instead of a period. The semicolon no conjunction (NC) rule is best applied when two sentences are closely related, especially when one or both sentences are short.

Rule 2: Semicolon Transition (TR)

Use a semicolon before and a comma after an adverbial conjunction when it acts as a bridge or transition between two independent clauses. This rule applies when adverbial conjunctions provide bridges between independent clauses; the semicolon implies the clauses are related in meaning.

> **semicolon TR:** Hernandez and Nichols will write the agenda; *however*, they are open to suggestions.

When writers avoid semicolons, they sometimes use commas incorrectly, resulting in a *run-on* sentence:

> **incorrect:** Hernandez and Nichols will write the agenda, *however*, they are open to suggestions.

In this example, correct the run-on by placing a semicolon or a period at the end of the first clause. Whenever an adverbial conjunction appears in the middle of a sentence, identify each independent clause; read through the sentence at least twice to ensure your punctuation is correct.

In the following examples adverbial conjunctions are shown in italics.

> Alexander and Chan wrote the grant; *therefore*, they should be on the committee.

> The grant was accepted; *as a result*, we will receive funding.

> You should call their office; *however*, (you) do not leave a message.

Rule 3: Semicolons Because of Commas (BC)

When a clause needs major and minor separations, use semicolons for major breaks and commas for minor breaks. Major and minor breaks don't occur very often when the writer keeps sentences simple, clear, and concise. Most often this rule applies when several cities and states or names and titles are listed:

semicolon BC: Goldblum will make presentations in Chicago, Illinois; Atlanta, Georgia; and Boston, Massachusetts.

semicolon BC: The committee members are Joe Clark, director of research; Mya Gonzalez, team leader; and Carson Michaels, research analyst.

The following example includes major and minor clauses within a sentence.

semicolon BC: Mickelson asked to address the committee; but since time was limited, it could not be scheduled.

semicolon BC: Professor Jones requested that the project continue; and I was unable to participate, so Dr. Ferretti was appointed.

Colons

In general, the colon alerts readers that information will be illustrated, making it a strong mark of punctuation that commands attention. Use colons for the following purposes:

1. After salutations of business letters and formal e-mail messages.
2. At the end of one sentence when the following sentence illustrates it.
3. At the end of a sentence to alert the reader that a list follows.
4. In ratios and proportions.
5. After words such as "Note" or "Caution."

Each of these categories is discussed in the following sections.

Colons After Salutations

A common use of a colon is after the salutation in a business letter, which is the most formal type of written communication. For professional letters, use "Dear" followed by a colon.

Dear Dr. Wilson:

Dear Professor:

Dear Keila:

Jorge:

You could also use these salutations in an e-mail if the message were formal, such as an inquiry for a job. However, for the most part, business professionals use a comma after the greeting of an e-mail.

Deion,   Hi Sophie,

The punctuation mark you should never use for a salutation is the semicolon; however, some writers mistakenly use it.

incorrect: Dear Charles;

correct: Dear Charles:

incorrect: Kenneth;

correct: Kenneth,

Colons After Sentences

Use a colon at the end of one sentence when the following sentence illustrates it. This type of colon use adds a nice element to writing style, conveying the message in a slightly more emphatic way. APA guidelines recommend always capitalizing the first word after the colon when a full sentence follows it.

Here is the principle that applies: A colon can be used in place of a period when the sentence that follows illustrates the one that precedes it.

Clinical psychologists should submit their reports by Friday: The accrediting commission's site visit is next week.

In general usage, the first word of the independent clause following a colon can be in lowercase, unless the second clause is a formal rule.

When you use a colon to illustrate a sentence, use it sparingly. While no rule applies, limit yourself to using no more than one or two colons per page to illustrate sentences this way.

Colons to Illustrate Lists

Using a colon to illustrate a list of words or phrases generally requires using words such as "these," "here," "the following," or "as follows" within a complete sentence.

These are the documents to bring: the reports for this year and last.

Bring the following identification: driver's license, passport, or photo ID.

Here are feedback samples that you can use: Myers, Jones, and Riley.

However, do not use a colon after an incomplete sentence.

incorrect: The categories you should use are: age, weight, and height.

correct: The categories you should use are age, weight, and height.

incorrect: This attachment includes: a list of participants and lodging assignments.

correct: This attachment includes a list of participants and lodging assignments.

Also notice that a colon can be used after the adverbial conjunction "for example" to alert the reader that an example follows.

Colons in Ratios and Proportions

Use a colon to separate numbers showing proportions; do not space before or after the colon.

For best results, use a 3:1 proportion of vinegar to water.

Colons After "Note" or "Caution"

Use a colon after "Note" or "Caution," and space only one time after the colon. Capitalize the first word after "Note" or "Caution," as shown in these examples:

Note: All meetings are cancelled on Friday.

Caution: Do not use the staircase.

However, for figure and table notes, APA recommends the use of a period after "Note" rather than a colon.

The Dash

The dash is the most versatile of all punctuation marks: it can substitute for a comma, semicolon, period, or colon. Use dashes for both formal and informal documents, but do not overuse them. In fact, there are two types of dashes: the *em dash* and the *en dash*. APA style employs both styles of dashes.

Em Dash

For general writing, the em dash is the traditional choice. Use two hyphens without a space before, between, or after them. When you key in a dash as two hyphens without spaces, your computer software will display the em dash as one solid line (about the width of a capital "m").

> The trial period ended on Friday—the research assistant said the results would arrive by noon today.

> Depression—not borderline personality disorder—was associated with increased risk.

The em dash adds energy, placing emphasis on the information that follows one dash or falls between two dashes. However, when overused, it gives the impression that the writer is speaking in a choppy and haphazard fashion.

En Dash

The en dash is often used when giving scores, directions, page numbers, or other information involving numbers. The en dash can also be used to separate words of equal weight. To create an en dash, key in one (or two) hyphens, placing a space before and after the hyphen; after the en dash appears, remove the space before and after it. This style of en dash will be slightly shorter than the em dash.

incorrect: See pages 189 – 204 for required qualifications.

correct: See pages 189–204 for required qualifications.

Here are a few more examples of the en dash:

Please complete items 1–10 before proceeding to the next section.

The convention will convene April 26–29.

The author–date citation needed to be added to the second paragraph.

Use hyphens, not dashes, in abbreviations for tests and scales, such as "t-test validity" or "DAS-II." Though a dash can be formed using hyphens on some word processors, a hyphen should not be substituted for a dash.

Once again, do not overuse dashes; using too many dashes is similar to using too many exclamation points. Writers enjoy using them, but readers tire of them easily. Thus, use them sparingly by limiting yourself to no more than one or two dashes per page or e-mail message.

Recap

Punctuation is an important tool not only to help you connect with your reader but also to give your message credibility. Work with punctuation until you feel confident using the various marks correctly. Experiment with semicolons, colons, and dashes until you gain a sense of how to use them effectively to express your voice.

WRITING WORKSHOP

Part 1: Editing Sentences

Instructions: Edit the following sentences, placing semicolons, colons, and dashes where needed.

1. Thank you for meeting with me regarding the position at JVTC Corporation I appreciated the opportunity to learn more about the company.

2. I am looking for a position in the medical field, and in the meantime I will further my education.

3. Thank you again for the chance to meet with you I wish you the best as you search for a great candidate for the position.

4. I am writing this letter to formally resign from my position at JVTC Corporation my last day will be May 13.

5. Please let me know what I can do to make sure the transition process goes smoothly I am willing to train and assist new employees as I finish up any projects I have.

Part 2: Editing a Thank You Letter

Instructions: Edit the following thank you letter, adding commas, semicolons, colons, and dashes, as needed. Also break the letter into paragraphs so that your letter contains a brief introduction, body, and conclusion.

Thank you for meeting with me on April 13 it was fascinating learning about you and the nursing position at your hospital. Your stories especially how writing and technology changed through the years was so interesting to learn about. The insight into the different types of writing you do daily gave me a newfound appreciation and expectation towards writing in the medical field. Thank you for sharing some insight into what you do I wish you all the best in your career.

Sincerely,

ACTIVITY KEYS

Semicolons, Colons, and Dashes

Part 1: Editing Sentences

Note: Answers may vary.

1. Thank you for meeting with me regarding the position at JVTC Corporation; I appreciated the opportunity to learn more about the company.

2. I am looking for a position in the medical field; and in the meantime, I will further my education.

3. Thank you again for the chance to meet with you—I wish you the best as you search for a great candidate for the position.

4. I am writing this letter to formally resign from my position at JVTC Corporation; my last day will be May 13.

5. Please let me know what I can do to make sure the transition process goes smoothly: I am willing to train and assist new employees as I finish up any projects I have.

Part 2. Editing a Thank You Letter

Note: Answers may vary.

[Dateline]

[Inside Address]

[Salutation:]

Thank you for meeting with me on April 13—it was fascinating learning about you and the nursing position at your hospital.

Your stories, especially how writing and technology changed through the years, were so interesting to learn about. The insight into the different types of writing you do daily gave me a newfound appreciation and expectation towards writing in the medical field.

Thank you for sharing some insight into what you do; I wish you all the best in your career.

Sincerely,

[Your Typed Signature]

Author Note: M. Ellis, BSN major at Indiana University Northwest, contributed to this chapter.

11

ACTIVE VOICE AND PARALLEL STRUCTURE

Academic writing is known for being passive and, at times, writers have valid reasons for using passive voice. However, writing experts and APA style recommend using active voice over passive voice, when possible; active voice conveys meaning in a clearer, simpler style. By using active voice, you are developing an effective writing style in line with APA's recommendations.

Another important quality of effective writing is parallel structure. For example, when writing sounds choppy and disjointed, check to see if it is lacking parallel structure. Parallel structure involves expressing similar sentence elements in the same grammatical form, creating balance, rhythm, and flow. As a result, parallel structure adds clarity and enhances understanding, which readers appreciate.

Speakers and writers use parallelism to draw attention to their point. On a micro level, parallel structure involves the syntax of individual sentences. On a macro level, parallel structure involves using repetitive phrases or sentences to draw in readers and build their expectations. For example, consider the parallel features of Dr. Martin Luther King's "I Have a Dream" speech. Dr. King's repetition added an indelible rhythm to his speech. When you listen to an especially effective speech, consider whether the speaker uses parallel repetition.

When you complete this chapter, you will be able to

* use active voice to shape writing so that it is clear and direct,

- identify nominalizations and turn them back into active verbs,
- apply passive voice in situations that call for tact,
- write sentences and bulleted lists using parallel structure,
- use the imperative voice when writing instructions, and
- write job duties using active verbs in parallel structure on a résumé.

APA Style, Active Voice, and Tone

Academic writing has a reputation of being passive, over-nominalized, and abstract—in other words, much academic writing is not reader friendly because it is more complicated than it needs to be. In contrast, APA guidelines recommend active, clear, concise, readable writing for academic papers. Let's take a look at how to apply active voice to your writing.

Active and Passive Voice

Though active voice is generally the voice of choice, passive voice has a necessary place in all types of writing when used *purposely*. For example, in scientific writing, the passive voice is used to place focus on a method or procedure rather than the person performing the action.

In general, active voice is preferred because passive voice can obscure meaning; the passive verb does not perform action, and its subject is a grammatical place holder, not a real subject that drives action:

- **With passive voice,** the verb describes action.
- **With active voice,** the verb performs action.

To further complicate meaning, passive writing also encourages the use of *nominalizations*, or verbs that have been transformed into their noun forms (see p. 219). When writers revise nominalizations back into active verbs, writing comes to life, and meaning becomes more easily accessible. However, in academic writing, passive voice coupled with nominalization is common; writers become attached to complicated writing, thinking long sentences and big words make them "sound smarter," when the opposite is often true: the best writers present even complex ideas in a simple, straightforward way.

Grammatical Subjects Versus Real Subjects

Since real subjects play a deciding role in the active voice, the following is a review of the difference between grammatical subjects and real subjects. *Real subjects* (RS) drive the action of verbs; however, the *grammatical subject* (GS) of a sentence is not always its real subject:

- The grammatical subject precedes the verb.
- The real subject drives the action of the verb.

When the RS precedes the verb, the RS and GS are the same.

Rupert's <u>director</u> gave them a project.

> GS/RS

However, in the following sentence, the real subject ("director") is not the grammatical subject ("Rupert").

<u>Rupert</u> was given a project by their <u>director</u>.

> GS   RS

Since the real subject appears in the sentence, this example is considered a *full passive*. In comparison, the following sentence has a grammatical subject but not a real subject.

A <u>project</u> was given to Rupert.

> GS

Who gave Rupert the project? Based on this sentence, we do not know. When a passive sentence does not contain a real subject, it is called a *truncated passive*.

Active Voice

The *active voice* is the most clear, direct, and concise way to phrase a sentence because each part of the sentence fills its prescribed role. The structure for the active voice is "Who did/does/will do what," while the structure for *passive voice* is "What was done/is done/will be done by whom."

Let us start with a passive sentence and then revise it to active voice.

passive: The contract was sent to our department by their grants office.

To change this passive sentence to active voice, first identify the main verb: "sent." Next, identify the real subject by asking who performed the action: Who sent the contract? According to the example, "their grants office" performed the action. Finally, change the order in the sentence so that the real subject (grants office) is also the grammatical subject.

active: Their grants office sent the contract to our department.

Here are the steps to change a sentence from passive voice to active voice:

1. Identify the main verb.
2. Identify the real subject by asking, "Who performed the action of the verb?"
3. Place the real subject (along with modifying words) at the beginning of the sentence, which is the position of the grammatical subject.
4. Follow the real subject with the verb, adjusting for agreement.
5. Complete the sentence.

In a shorter form, here is the process:

Step 1: Main verb?

Step 2: Real subject?

Steps 3 and 4: Real subject + verb (agreement and tense?)

Step 5: S – V – O

The following is another example of a sentence revised from passive voice to active voice.

passive: The conference was scheduled by the department chair.

step 1: main verb: "scheduled"

step 2: real subject: "department chair"

steps 3 and 4: real subject + verb: "The department chair scheduled"

step 5: complete sentence: "The department chair scheduled the conference."

This step-by-step process makes revising sentences from passive voice to active voice sound simple. In fact, the process is simple, even with complex sentences. The challenges arise when you start revising your own writing because you also need to revise your thinking.

At first, it may be difficult to identify sentences you have written in the passive voice. That's partly because writing in a complicated way is familiar to you and feels comfortable. Reading your own writing also feels comfortable because you are already familiar with your ideas. A place to start is noticing your reaction as a reader to multiple types of writing others produce so that you can analyze your own writing with an open mind.

Passive Voice: The Tactful Voice

Since the real subject does not need to be present in a passive sentence, the following are times when passive voice is preferred over active voice:

- Whenever you do not want to focus on a specific person because it would be more tactful not to sound accusatory, use passive voice.

  passive: An error was made in the calculation.

Who made the error? An active sentence needs an actor or agent performing the action of its verb; however, a passive sentence does not need an actor or agent because its verb does not create action.

- Whenever you do not know who performed an action, use passive voice.

  passive: The laptop was taken from the storeroom.

Using a *truncated passive* is natural and necessary when the real subject is not known. While truncated passives play a vital role in writing, using them when they are unnecessary interferes with the quality and flow of writing.

Nominalization

Verbs that change forms to function as nouns are called *nominals.* The actual term for transforming a verb into a noun is *nominalization.* When writers revise nominalizations back into active verbs, writing comes to life, and meaning becomes more easily accessible.

Many verbs commonly turn into nominalizations by adding the suffix "–ment" or "–tion." For example, "define" turns into "definition," and "commit" turns into "commitment." Table 11.1 presents a few more examples.

TABLE 11.1   Verb Nominalizations

Verb	Nominal
accomplish	accomplishment
decide	decision
develop	development
evaluate	evaluation
facilitate	facilitation
verify	verification

Do you see how the nominalized version is a longer, more complex word? Nominalization removes action from a verb, and when writers use nominalizations unnecessarily, their writing becomes more complicated.

Here is an example of the verb "appreciate" used in its nominalized form: "appreciation."

nominalized: I want to express my appreciation for your help.

active: I appreciate your help.

When writers refuse to give up nominalizations and the passive voice, they may mistakenly believe that they sound sophisticated. Unnecessarily long four-syllable words do not improve the flow of writing. Follow Leonard DaVinci's advice on the topic: "Simplicity is the ultimate sophistication."

As an effective writer, make complex messages as simple as you can. Use nominalizations only when they improve the efficiency of your writing, and use passive voice only when it improves the tone of your writing.

The following is another example showing passive voice and nominalizations used together.

nominalized: Encouragement was given to me by my coach and teammates.

passive: I was encouraged by my coach and teammates.

active: My coach and teammates encouraged me.

In the first sentence in the example, the nominalization "encouragement" is used in a passive sentence. In the second, the nominal is removed, but the sentence is still passive. In the third, "encourage" is used as an active verb in its past tense form.

Understanding these principles is much easier than actually applying them to your own writing. To achieve active writing, you need to be committed; the more committed you are, the more improvement you will make in your writing.

Parallel Structure

When writing sounds choppy and disjointed, check to see if it is lacking *parallel structure*. Parallel structure involves expressing similar sentence elements in the same grammatical form, creating balance, rhythm, and flow. As a result, parallel structure adds clarity and enhances understanding, which readers appreciate.

Parallel structure is an important element in writing clear instructions as well as listing consistent bullet points on your résumé. When editing sentences, look for parallel structure with the following:

- items in a series (nouns, adjectives, and phrases)
- clauses and tenses
- correlative conjunctions

Items in a Series

Writers have various ways of shifting structure when using nouns, thereby losing parallel structure.

> **inconsistent:** The meeting was long, boring, and the topic didn't interest me.

> **parallel:** The meeting was long, boring, and uninteresting. (adjectives)

Another common way to lose parallel structure is shifting from infinitives to gerunds. Infinitives and gerunds are nominals, so they function as nouns, not as verbs. For parallel structure, the key to using gerunds and infinitives is using one or the other but not both.

> **inconsistent:** Fred is going to write the report, edit it, and then submitting it to the committee.

> **parallel:** Fred is going to write the report, edit it, and then submit it to the committee. (nouns/infinitives)

> **inconsistent:** The program is short, intense, and many people like it.

> **parallel:** The program is short, intense, and popular. (adjectives)

Phrases

Parallel agreement with phrases can be tricky, especially with prepositional phrases. For example, a preposition may not fit all of the phrases that follow it, necessitating the addition of a preposition that would fit.

> **inconsistent:** Our mission is understanding patient needs, customizing solutions, and the provision of individualized plans.

> **parallel:** Our mission is understanding patient needs, customizing solutions, and providing individualized plans.

> **inconsistent:** The report listed members of the task force and the data collection.

> **parallel:** The report listed members of the task force and information about the data collection.

You may find a prepositional phrase followed by another type of structure:

inconsistent: The participants received an award for their commitment and because they are motivated.

parallel: The participants received an award for their commitment and [for] their motivation.

inconsistent: Of the people surveyed, the responses indicated that they received better individualized care and also a higher quality of life.

parallel: Of the people surveyed, their responses indicated that they received better individualized care and that they also experienced a higher quality of life.

Clauses

When a sentence shifts from active voice to passive voice, or vice versa, the sentence lacks parallel structure.

inconsistent: Nurses working excessively long shifts experience stress, and sometimes burnout is suffered as a result. (active–passive)

parallel: Nurses working excessively long shifts experience stress, and they sometimes suffer burnout. (active–active)

inconsistent: The hospital increased our budget, so a program was developed to improve intake. (active–passive)

parallel: The hospital increased our budget, so we developed a program to improve intake. (active–active)

Tenses

Do not shift verb tense unnecessarily. In other words, stay in present tense or past tense, unless the meaning of the sentence requires that you change tense.

inconsistent: The workshop trains nurses in offsite deliveries and was completed last week.

parallel: The workshop trained nurses in offsite deliveries and was completed last week.

inconsistent: The manual states that calling in sick in emergencies was accepted only for special circumstances.

parallel: The manual states that calling in sick in emergencies is accepted only for special circumstances.

Correlative Conjunctions

The following are common pairs of conjunctions—notice that the second word in the pair is a coordinating conjunction.

either ... or	not ... but
neither ... nor	not only ... but also
both ... and	whether ... or

When using correlative conjunctions, follow the second part of the correlative with the same structure as the first part.

inconsistent: Our department either is giving excellent service or no service at all.

parallel: Our department is either giving excellent service or giving no service at all.

inconsistent: Neither the staff was available to handle the situation nor the administration.

parallel: Neither was the staff available to handle the situation nor was the administration.

inconsistent: The data not only show increased infection rates but also are providing long-term injury statistics.

parallel: The data not only show increased infection rates but also provide long-term injury statistics.

Lists and the Imperative Voice

When displaying lists, you can use various styles, but remain consistent. For example, you can display items using active voice, nouns, gerund phrases, or infinitive phrases.

However, when you write a list of instructions, the most effective style is the *imperative mood* or *voice*, which makes a command or request. The imperative voice communicates to the reader what must be done in the most simple, direct way; for example, the imperative voice occurs in the second person, and the subject is "you": (you) attend the meeting, and (you) *take* notes. (The imperative voice is equivalent to active voice in second person.)

The following is an incorrect, inconsistent list, which is then displayed in the various corrected styles:

1. development of effective communication skills
2. conflict resolution among the group
3. recruitment of project leaders
4. increasing diversity in committees
5. coaching effective job performance

The following list has been corrected using verbs in active or imperative voice:

1. Develop effective communication skills.
2. Resolve conflict among the group.
3. Recruit project leaders.
4. Increase diversity in committees.
5. Coach effective job performance.

The following list has been corrected using gerund phrases:

1. developing effective communication skills
2. resolving conflict among the group
3. recruiting project leaders
4. increasing diversity in committees

5. coaching effective job performance

The following list has been corrected using infinitive phrases:

1. to develop effective communication skills
2. to resolve conflict among the group
3. to recruit project leaders
4. to increase diversity in committees
5. to coach effective job performance

WRITING TIP

APA: Bulleted Lists and Capitalization

For bulleted lists, APA (2020) recommends the following:

- If the list consists of words or phrases, start each item with a lowercase letter.
- If the list consists of complete sentences, capitalize the first word.

  Since other sources vary in the way capitalization is applied to bulleted and numbered lists, for professional writing, feel free to capitalize the first word of each item of a bulleted list. For example, for bulleted lists on your résumé, you may prefer to capitalize the first word of the bullet point, even for phrases. Regardless of the style you choose, make sure to apply *parallel structure* so that all items are in the same grammatical form.

Bulleted Lists on Résumés

Apply parallel structure when listing job duties on a résumé. Start each bullet with an active verb: for current positions, use present tense; for past positions, use past tense.

The following is a list of sample job duties for a current position:

- Develop and implement training programs

- Schedule and conduct interviews
- Prepare and organize schedules
- Negotiate contracts for temporary workers

The following is a list of sample job duties for a past position:

- Maintained status updates
- Supervised interns
- Planned and administered policy changes
- Secured funding for special projects
- Ensured compliance of federal standards

Recap

Using active voice improves the quality and readability of writing; active voice is clear, concise, and direct. Do the following to improve the quality of your writing:

- Shift passive sentences to active voice, whenever possible.
- Use passive voice for situations that call for tact.
- Turn nominalizations back to active verbs.
- Use parallel structure for lists and items on your résumé.

Parallel structure comes in all shapes and forms. Developing a keen eye for similar sentence elements takes time and commitment. As you focus attention on parallel structure, you will see connections you did not previously see.

Do the following to improve the quality of your writing:

- Express similar sentence elements in the same grammatical form: noun for noun, verb for verb, phrase for phrase, and clause for clause.
- Start bulleted lists with gerunds, infinitives, or verbs.
- Use the imperative voice when writing instructions (which is equivalent to using the active voice in second person).
- Use parallel structure when listing job duties on your résumé.

WRITING WORKSHOP

Parallel Lists

Instructions: The following is a list of job duties. Revise the list to reflect the job duties of a current position, and then revise the list to reflect job duties from a past job:

- Filing patient records
- Faxing and e-mail financial documents to clients
- Fax financial documents
- Tax resolution and letter preparation
- Utilization of QuickBooks, Oracle NetSuite, and FreshBooks
- Transportation of equipment between patient rooms
- Maintenance of clean and orderly areas
- Inspection and clean equipment
- Ensured serving areas are safe and sanitary
- Explained use and care of equipment
- Updating website with products, prices, and photos
- Assisting patients with bathing, medication, and feeding
- Entering monthly bank statements, receipts, and charge clips for monthly budget
- Tabulation of weekly inventory
- Preparation and organization of schedules
- Negotiation of contracts for outsourcing

ACTIVITY KEY

Parallel Lists

Edited for current position:

- File patient records
- Fax and e-mail financial documents to clients

- Resolve tax issues and prepare letters
- Use QuickBooks, Oracle NetSuite, and FreshBooks
- Transport equipment between patient rooms
- Maintain clean and orderly areas
- Inspect and clean equipment
- Ensure serving areas are safe and sanitary
- Explain use and care of equipment
- Update website with products, prices, and photos
- Assist patients with bathing, medication, and feeding
- Enter bank statements, receipts, and charge clips for monthly budget
- Tabulate weekly inventory
- Prepare and organize schedules
- Negotiate contracts for outsourcing

Edited for past position:

- Filed patient records
- Faxed and e-mailed financial documents to clients
- Resolved tax issues and prepared letters
- Used QuickBooks, Oracle NetSuite, and FreshBooks
- Transported equipment between patient rooms
- Maintained clean and orderly areas
- Inspected and cleaned equipment
- Ensured serving areas were safe and sanitary
- Explained use and care of equipment
- Updated website with products, prices, and photos
- Assisted patients with bathing, medication, and feeding
- Entered bank statements, receipts, and charge clips for monthly budget
- Tabulated weekly inventory

- Prepared and organized schedules
- Negotiated contracts for outsourcing

Reference

American Psychological Association. (2020). *Publication manual of the American Psychological Association* (7th ed.). https://doi.org/10.1037/0000165-000

12

CAPITALIZATION AND NUMBER USAGE

apitalization is an essential element of all academic and professional writing. APA follows standard rules for capitalization but also adds a few twists, such as their treatment of prepositions and the use of sentence case.

When writers are unsure of the rules, they have a tendency to capitalize too many words. And sometimes even when they are "sure" of the rules, they also capitalize too many words. By learning a few basic rules about capitalization, you can eliminate many errors in your writing ... and some of those basic rules may surprise you.

When you use numbers in a document, should they be written as words or numerals? Since writing in the social and physical sciences often involves numbers, you will be at an advantage by knowing the rules. For example, both quantitative research and qualitative research contain numbers. When you learn the rules for numbers, you will be able to make clear, consistent decisions so that your writing is correct and credible. The first section of this chapter reviews basic guidelines for capitalization, and the second section covers basic number usage.

When you complete this chapter, you will

- understand the difference between common nouns and proper nouns,
- be able to apply capitalization rules for sentence case and title case for APA style,

- be able to apply rules for capitalization for professional titles and academic degrees,
- be able to review capitalization rules for diseases and disorders,
- be able to distinguish between when to spell out numbers and when to use numerals, and
- know basic number rules, such as how to display ages, dates, percentages, and so on.

Capitalization

Whether you are writing a formal paper or a casual e-mail message, applying standard rules of capitalization gives your writing credibility. Since writers have the tendency to capitalize too many words, start by applying the general rule, "When in doubt, do not capitalize." Then when you are unsure, do a bit of research to learn the rule that applies. Before covering basic principles, the first part of this section covers details about capitalization that differ from the Modern Library Association (MLA) and *Chicago Manual of Style* (*CMoS*).

APA Style: Title Case and Sentence Case

For presenting titles, APA style employs two different types of capitalization styles: *title case* and *sentence case.* You are likely to be more familiar with title case, which is the traditional style for writing in general.

When using title case, type words in both uppercase and lowercase, following basic guidelines for capitalization. Capitalize all words in the title except for articles, conjunctions, and prepositions of three letters or fewer. Use title case for the following:

- the title of your paper (title page)
- all headings in your paper
- titles of books, periodicals, articles, chapters, and reports within the text of your paper
  - Italicize the titles of books and periodicals.
  - Use quotation marks around the titles of articles and chapters.
- titles of tables and figures
- the title of a journal on the reference page (APA 2020)

When using sentence case, capitalize the first word of the title and the first word following a colon (e.g., the subtitle) as well as proper nouns and proper adjectives; all other words are typed in lowercase. Use sentence case for the following:

- the titles of books, articles, and websites on the reference page
- table column headings

> **in text:** *Tuesdays With Morrie: An Old Man, a Young Man, and Life's Greatest Lesson*
>
> **reference list:** *Tuesdays with Morrie: An old man, a young man, and life's greatest lesson*

Articles, Conjunctions, and Prepositions in Titles

In titles of literary and artistic works, the following words would be capitalized only as the first word of a title or subtitle:

- **articles:** the a, and an
- **conjunctions:** and, but, or, nor, for, so, and yet
- **prepositions of three or fewer letters:** to, at, in, and for, among others

APA style requires prepositions of four or more letters to be capitalized, including "with," "from," "over," "before," "among," and "between."

> Tuesdays With Morrie (APA style)
>
> Tuesdays with Morrie (MLA style and *CMoS* style)

Thus, if the title of your paper contains a preposition that has four or more letters, capitalize the preposition:

> Coping Techniques Applied Among Nursing Students Under Stress

Proper Nouns Versus Common Nouns

Do you understand the difference between *proper nouns* and *common nouns*? A proper noun is the official name of a particular person, place, or thing, while a common noun is a general term that refers to a class of things. The first basic principle of capitalization is to capitalize proper nouns but set common nouns in lowercase (see Table 12.1).

TABLE 12.1 **Proper Nouns Versus Common Nouns**

Proper Noun	Common Noun
American Psychological Association	psychologist therapist biologist
Bachelor of Science in Psychology	bachelor's degree in psychology
John Wilson	name person friend business associate
Wilson Corporation	company corporation business

Capitalize the official name of a department, but not an unofficial name (see Table 12.2). The official name of a department may be different from the way to which it is commonly referred, and names of departments can vary from college to college. For example, the psychology department at your college may be the "Department of Psychology," or it may be the "Psychology Department." Check with individual institutions, and capitalize only the official version.

Schedule an appointment with the chair of your psychology department.

Schedule an appointment with the chair of the Department of Psychology.

Capitalize official course titles but not subjects and majors.

TABLE 12.2 **Course Names Versus Subjects or Majors**

Course Name	Subject or Major
Introduction to Clinical Psychology	clinical psychology psychology major
Introduction to Criminal Justice	criminal justice major
Concepts in Mental Health	mental health

Capitalize the names of unique places and things (see Table 12.3).

TABLE 12.3 **Capitalization of Different Noun Types**

Type of Noun	Capitalization
Titles of literary and artistic works	*The Daily Beast*
Racial and ethnic terms	Hispanic
	Asian
	African American
	Appalachian
	European
Words derived from proper nouns	English
	South American
Organization names	American Psychological Association
	International Sociological Association
Brand and trade names	Tesla
	Microsoft
Points of the compass	north
	west
	northwest
Specific geographic regions	the West
	the American South
	the Southwest
Periods of time and historical events	Great Depression
	Information Age
Days of the week, months, and holidays	Thanksgiving
	Christmas
	Chanukah
	Kwanzaa
	Veterans Day

Capitalize proper adjectives derived from proper nouns (see Table 12.4).

TABLE 12.4 **Capitalization of Different Noun Types**

Proper Noun	Derivative or Proper Adjective
England	English language
Spain	Spanish olive oil
Africa	African pottery
Asia	Asian food

First Words

Capitalize the first word of each of the following:

* sentences (including the first word of a complete sentence following a colon)
* poems
* direct quotations that are complete sentences
* independent questions within a sentence
* the first word of a complete sentence that follows a word of instruction or caution, such as "Note" or "Caution"

For APA style, do not capitalize the following:

* the first word of a bulleted list of phrases or sentence fragments
* a proper noun that begins with a lowercase letter, even when the name is the first word of a sentence, such as "von Dorn"

Diseases and Disorders

The names of diseases, disorders, and therapies are not proper nouns and should not be capitalized. However, when a personal name is used within the name, capitalize the name (APA, 2020).

Do not capitalize the following examples:

cancer	allergies
autism spectrum disorder	diarrhea
diabetes mellitus	mononucleosis
diabetes type 2	chronic obstructive pulmonary
high blood pressure	disease

Capitalize the names in the following examples:

Alzheimer's disease	Bright's disease
Parkinson's disease	Addison's disease
Lou Gehrig's disease	Tay-Sachs disease
Chron's disease	Asperberger's syndrome
Huntington's disease	non-Hodgkin's lymphoma
Tourette syndrome	Creutzfeld-Jakob disease

These lists are a small sampling of diseases and disorders; when in doubt, check to see if the term includes a person's name or proper noun, which would be capitalized.

Professional Titles Versus Occupations

Some writers capitalize all titles, thinking a title is a proper noun; however, titles are not proper nouns.

> **incorrect:** José Barton, Academic Dean, will meet with us today.

> **correct:** José Barton, academic dean, will meet with us today.

> **correct:** Dean Barton will meet with us today.

Can you see the subtle differences in how the terms are used?
The following are general guidelines related to titles:

- Capitalize titles when they precede a name.

   Professor Hernandez will take care of the matter.

   You can speak with Professor Ferretti at 3 p.m.

- Do not capitalize titles when they follow a name.

   Rose Bornstein, director of admissions, will assist you.

   They sent the letter to A. S. Ferretti, professor, at his Rome address.

- Capitalize a title used in a direct address without the person's name.

   Thank you, Professor, for responding.

   Would you, Doctor, give the information to my assistant?

- Do not capitalize titles when they are used to refer to occupations.

   chancellor

   president

   vice president

executive director

chief financial officer

professor

dean

instructor

academic advisor

Abbreviations, Acronyms, and Initialisms

An *acronym* is a form of abbreviation formed from the initial letters of words and pronounced as one word, such as the following:

AWOL: absent without official leave

AIDS: acquired immunodeficiency syndrome

An *initialism* is an abbreviation formed from a string of initials and generally pronounced as individual letters, such as the following:

APA: American Psychological Association

AANP: American Association of Nurse Practitioners

While acronyms and initialisms are written in all-capital letters, abbreviations are not. However, if the abbreviation is derived from a foreign word, it may be set in italics.

Academic Degrees and Capitalization

When referring to academic degrees in general terms, do not capitalize them.

bachelor's degree

master's degree

doctor's degree

master of science

bachelor of arts

bachelor's in radiology

When using the full name of a degree, capitalize it:

Bachelor of Science in Nursing

Master of Science in Dental Hygiene

When the name of the degree follows a personal name, capitalize it, whether it is written in full or abbreviated. When a degree is abbreviated, APA advises against using periods. However, you can use periods for general purposes, if you prefer. As always, a key to good writing is being consistent.

Florence Nightingale, Master of Science in Nursing

Florence Nightingale, MSN

Hyphenated Words

At times, you will need to determine how to capitalize hyphenated words for titles and works. For general writing and APA style, capitalize each word of a hyphenated term used in a *title* (except short prepositions and conjunctions, as previously noted).

Up-to-Date Reports

Mid-July Conference

Long-Term Outlook

Nouns Followed by Numerals or Letters

Capitalize nouns followed by numerals or letters.

Table 1

Appendix A

Research Question 2

Two Common Capitalization Errors

Some writers have become lax with their use of capitalization because of the prevalence of texting and social media posting. However, it's important not to carry those types of errors over to academic and professional writing. Writing that is grammatically correct garners far more respect than writing that is riddled with errors.

In addition, much professional writing goes into permanent records, which are legal documents. At times, court cases have been lost due to poor record keeping that is full of errors. With that in mind, follow these guidelines to avoid common capitalization errors:

1. Always capitalize the personal pronoun "I."

   incorrect: A friend asked me if i could help, so i said that i would.

   correct: A friend asked if I could help, so I said that I would.

2. Do not write using all UPPERCASE or all lowercase.

Writers who are unsure about writing decisions make these kinds of errors. In fact, using all uppercase has commonly come to mean that the writer is shouting, which often is not the case.

Using all lowercase sometimes reflects a tradition within certain professional niches, such as technical professionals. When communicating to professionals outside of their inner circle, even technical professionals would enhance communication by applying standard rules of capitalization.

Number Usage

This section includes general guidelines for basic number rules, focusing on APA usage. However, APA style covers a vast array of diverse number rules that apply to research writing. When you do advanced work and deal with numbers, review number rules directly in the *Publication Manual of the American Psychological Association*, 7th Edition (2020).

Spelling Out Numbers

Spell out numbers in words for the following:

- numbers zero through nine within written text
- ordinal numbers one through nine, such as "first," "second," and so on
- The first word of a sentence, such as "Fifty participants were present."
  - Alternatively, you can reword the sentence so that the number is not the first word.
- Centuries that are single digit, spell out, such as "ninth century"; for double-digit centuries, the preference for APA is to use numerals, such as "19th century"
  - Note that MLA and CMoS advise spelling out the names of centuries.
- Common fractions, such as one half

Using Numerals for Numbers

Use numerals for the following:

- numbers 10 and above within written text
- ordinal numbers 10 and above, such as "10th," "15th," and so on
- references to tables

Table 5

Figure 3

- precise units of measurement

2 mm

2 inches

- statistical or mathematical functions, proportions, and ratios

6 divided by 2

5 times as many graduates

3 of the 4 applicants (proportion)

a ratio of 3:1

- numbered series, parts of books, and tables

  pages 53–64

- a sample size or specific number of participants

  7 participants

- percentages
  - Use the percent symbol after a numeral

  10%

  - Use the word "percent" after any number expressed as a word, such as a number that begins a sentence, title, or text heading:

  Five percent of the returns … .

  - Use the word "percentage," not "percent," when no number appears with it

  A high percentage of participants responded.

- ages

  The sample included 9- to 12-year-olds.

  The participants of the study were 21 years old.

- Exact sums of money

  $15.92

Large Numbers

Numbers in the millions or higher can be written as a combination of numerals and words if the number can be expressed as a whole number or as a whole number plus a simple fraction or decimal amount.

The grant request was for $1.5 million, but we received $1.2 million.

Plurals of Numbers

When forming plurals of numbers, do not add an apostrophe.

The research was done in the 1960s.

Decimal Fractions

For numbers less than 1, use a "0" before the decimal point if the number can be greater than 1.

0.9 mm

For numbers less than 1, do not use a "0" before the decimal point if the number *cannot be* greater than 1.

$p = .041$

Dates and Time

- Spell out the names of months; use figures for days.

September 4, 2019

February 2020

- Use figures for time, and use the abbreviations "a.m." and "p.m." or the word "o'clock" but not both.

4 p.m.

4 o'clock in the afternoon

- For time on the hour, you may omit the :00.
- Use the ordinal ending for dates only when the day precedes the month.

21st of February

Back-to-Back Modifiers

Use a combination of numerals and words to express back-to-back modifiers.

The Beck Depression scale has four 10-point subscales.

Indefinite Numbers

Write indefinite numbers, such as "thousands" or "hundreds," in words.

We were pleased with the hundreds of positive responses.

Phone Numbers

Display phone numbers by using parentheses around the area code or by using a hyphen or period between parts.

> **incorrect:** (212)555-1212 *or* 2125551212
>
> **correct:** (212) 555-1212, 212-555-1212, or 212.555.1212

Recap

Rules create standards so that everyone can understand the meaning of the message, reducing confusion and misunderstanding. By following some important rules regarding capitalization and numbers, you improve the quality of your writing as well your credibility as a writer:

- Capitalize proper nouns but not common nouns.
- Always capitalize the personal pronoun "I."
- Capitalize a business title when it precedes a person's name but not when it follows the name.
- In general, the names of diseases and disorders are not capitalized, unless a personal name is used within the name.
- Do not capitalize occupations or job positions.
- Spell out numbers one through nine; use figures for numbers 10 and above.

By writing correctly, you show respect for your readers, enhancing relationships as well as your ability to communicate across borders and continents.

WRITING WORKSHOP

Capitalizing Book and Article Titles in APA Style

Instructions: For the following, show how the title would be displayed in APA style, first as an in-text reference and then as a formal reference on the reference page.

1. **book title:** Prevent and Reverse Heart Disease

   in text:

   reference page:

2. **book title:** How Not to Die: Discover the Foods Scientifically Proven to Prevent and Reverse Disease

   in text:

   reference:

3. **article title:** HIPAA Regulations: A New Era of Medical-Record Privacy

   in text:

   reference page:

4. **article title:** Food as Medicine: Preventing and Treating the Most Common Diseases with Diet

   in text:

   reference page:

5. **website title:** Physicians Committee for Responsible Medicine (pcrm.org)

   in text:

   reference page:

6. **website title:** NutritionFacts.org

   in text:

   reference page:

ACTIVITY KEY

Capitalizing Book and Article Titles in APA Style

1. **book title:** Prevent and Reverse Heart Disease

   in text: *Prevent and Reverse Heart Disease*

   reference page: *Prevent and reverse heart disease*

2. **book title:** How Not to Die: Discover the Foods Scientifically Proven to Prevent and Reverse Disease

in text: *How Not to Die: Discover the Foods Scientifically Proven to Prevent and Reverse Disease*

reference page: *How not to die: Discover the foods scientifically proven to prevent and reverse disease*

3. **article title:** HIPAA Regulations: A New Era of Medical-Record Privacy

   in text: "HIPAA Regulations: A New Era of Medical-Record Privacy"

   reference page: HIPAA regulations: A new era of medical-record privacy

4. **article title:** Food as Medicine: Preventing and Treating the Most Common Diseases with Diet

   in text: "Food as Medicine: Preventing and Treating the Most Common Diseases with Diet"

   reference page: Food as medicine: Preventing and treating the most common diseases with diet

5. **website title:** Physicians Committee for Responsible Medicine (pcrm.org)

   in text: Physicians Committee for Responsible Medicine (pcrm.org)

   reference page: Physicians Committee for Responsible Medicine (pcrm.org)

6. **website title:** NutritionFacts.org

   in text: NutritionFacts.org

   reference page: NutritionFacts.org

Reference

American Psychological Association. (2020). *Publication manual of the American Psychological Association* (7th ed.). https://doi.org/10.1037/0000165-000

GLOSSARY OF TERMS

A

abstract: a short, written statement no longer than 250 words that gives an overview of a report, study, or proposal; usually associated with scientific studies but equivalent to an executive summary or a synopsis.

academic writing: a formal style of writing in which a thesis statement is used to develop the introduction, body, and conclusion; it characterizes research papers, arguments, essays, and creative writing. Compare **business writing**.

acronym: an abbreviation pronounced as a word (e.g., AARP and SADD).

action verb: a verb that transfers action from a subject to an object; in English, all verbs except 11 linking verbs. Also see **state-of-being verb**.

active listening: a listening skill that involves focusing on the meaning, intent, and feelings of the person who is speaking to gain a clear understanding of the message.

active voice: as applied to verbs, a term indicating that the subject performs the action of the verb (e.g., "Bob *wrote* the report"). Compare **passive voice**.

adjective: a word that modifies a noun or pronoun.

adverbial conjunction: a word or phrase (e.g., "however," "therefore," and "thus") that serves as a transition between sentences or paragraphs; shows the relationship between ideas and plays a significant role in punctuation.

annotated bibliography: a list of citations to books, articles, and documents that includes a brief description and evaluation, generally consisting of a 100–150-word summary of the relevance, accuracy, and quality of each resource.

antecedent: the word or words to which a pronoun refers.

appositive: a restatement; a brief explanation that identifies the noun or pronoun preceding it. See also **essential appositive**.

auxiliary (verb): a verb (e.g., any form of "be," "have," or "do") used with an-other verb to convey a different meaning or tense. Also called a "helper" verb.

B

background thinking: a person's thoughts about how they arrived at a conclusion or how readers will interpret that conclusion; a type of meta-discourse that should be eliminated from writing.

bar chart: a graphics tool that displays information in vertical or horizontal bars; enables the reader to compare and contrast different items.

base form: the original state of a verb. See also **infinitive**.

base settings: setting paragraph controls at single spacing with no added space before or after paragraphs.

bibliography: a comprehensive list of the sources cited in a document (and sometimes of sources consulted but not cited); follows a standard format, including author, title of work, and publication or other identifying data for each work.

binary: in the context of gender, classifying gender in two distinct and oppo-site forms of masculine and feminine.

boundary: a hypothetical construct that defines the border that separates the system from its suprasystem; for example, personal boundaries and gener-ational boundaries.

business writing: a direct style of writing in which context is used to define the purpose of the message; it characterizes letters, memos, and e-mails that get to the point quickly. Key components are connecting with reader, re-lating main points, and clarifying action to be taken. Compare **academic writing**. See also **professional writing**.

C

case: in grammar, the function a pronoun performs in a sentence, such as subjective (or nominative), objective, possessive, and reflexive.

CARS model: a pattern identified by John Swales for writing an introduc-tion to a research paper; "creating a research space" includes three rhetorical moves: establishing a research territory, establishing a research niche, and occupying the niche.

CAT strategy: in e-mail messages, a structural approach (connect - act - tell) that connects with the reader, states desired action, and gives supportive information.

central idea: a thesis statement that expresses the main point of a paper.

Chicano: U.S. citizens of Mexican descent.

cisgender: a term used for individuals whose sex assigned at birth aligns with their gender identity.

cisgenderism: the belief that being cisgender is normative, as indicated by the assumption that individuals are cisgender unless otherwise specified.

cissexism: prejudice or discrimination against people who are transgender.

clarity: clearness and simplicity.

cliché: a fixed or stereotyped expression that has lost its significance through frequent repetition.

closing: (1) the last paragraph of a letter, stating action the recipient needs to take; (2) a complimentary sign-off (e.g., for letters, "Sincerely"; for e-mails "Best regards" or "All the best").

coherent: a term referring to a paragraph that presents a logical flow of ideas, developing a topic in a consistent, rational way. One idea leads to another.

cohesive: a term referring to a paragraph that presents one main topic along with details to support that topic, demonstrating connectedness among the ideas it contains. All ideas adhere together for a common purpose.

colloquial: informal, conversational language patterns that include slang and nonstandard English. See **idiom.**

colloquialism: a saying that is not taken literally; expresses an idea unique to specific time and location (e.g., "That dog can't hunt.").

colon: a traditional mark of punctuation; alerts the reader that information will follow that explains or illuminates the information that preceded it.

comma splice: a grammatical error in which two independent clauses are joined with only a comma, causing a run-on sentence.

comparative form: the form of an adjective used when two items are compared; for regular adjectives, it is formed by adding the suffix "-er" or using "more" or "less" before the adjective.

composing: creating, inventing, or discovering; planning or mapping your message; drafting your ideas on the page.

coordinating conjunction: a word that joins items of equal grammatical structure, such as independent clauses or items in a series. The seven coordinating conjunctions are "and," "but," "or," "nor," "for," "yet," and "so."

correlative conjunction: a pair of conjunctions (e.g., not only … but also) that compares or contrasts ideas. The information presented after each conjunction must be presented in the same grammatical form (i.e., parallel construction).

courteous request: in written communications, a question that prompts the recipient to act rather than respond in words; ends with a period rather than a question mark.

cover e-mail: for online job searches, an e-mail message that indicates an electronic résumé is attached and that summarizes the sender's interest in a company and requests an interview. Also see **cover letter** and **cover message**.

cover letter: (1) enclosed with a proposal, a letter summarizing key points in the proposal; (2) enclosed with a résumé, a letter that summarizes the senders interest in a company, highlights accomplishments, and requests an interview. Also called "application letter." Also see **cover e-mail**.

cover message: for sending documents as attachments via e-mail, a message that fulfils the same function as a cover letter.

credibility: believability; equates to trust, a critical element in all relationships.

critic's block: a barrier to writing that is caused by being too critical of one's ability to write well or improve writing skills.

cultural sensitivity: the dynamics of communication that relate to diversity, such as cultural, generational, gender, and personality differences.

D

dash: a substitute for the comma, semicolon, period, or colon used to emphasize the information that follows it; appropriate in both formal and informal documents.

dependent clause: a group of words that has a subject and verb but does not express a complete thought; cannot stand alone as a sentence.

direct address: the use of a person's name or title in addressing them directly.

direct approach: in written communications, a style that gets right to the point; conveys the purpose and main point in the first paragraph, followed by supporting information or details. Compare **indirect approach.**

DOI: a digital object identifier consists of a string of numbers, letters, and symbols to identify and permanently link an article or document and link it to its source on the internet. For APA style, when a resource includes a DOI, it does not need a "retrieved from" date in the citation information.

E

editing: improving the flow of writing by changing the wording and cutting unnecessary words to make the writing more concise and readable.

editing strategy: an approach to editing that focuses on turning passive, wordy writing into simple, clear, and concise writing.

editor's block: being overly concerned with product at the expense of process.

ellipsis marks: three spaced periods used to indicate the omission of a word or words from a quotation. (Add a fourth period if the ellipsis [plural "ellipses"] occurs at the end of a sentence.)

e-mail: electronic mail—the most widely used form of written communication; in business, used to communicate with colleagues in-house (on an intranet) or with associates outside of the company (on the Internet).

emphatic: an adjective or adverb used to place emphasis on the word it describes; can detract from the message rather than place emphasis on it, so should be used sparingly (e.g., "very," "really," and "incredible").

empty information: irrelevant or redundant information that adds nothing of value for your reader.

essential appositive: a word or phrase that identifies a particular person or thing in a sentence where the identity would not be clear without the appositive; should not be set off with commas.

essential element: any part of a sentence that cannot be removed without compromising meaning or structure; should not be set off with commas. Also called a "restrictive element."

evidence: proof of an assertion or research finding; typically consists of objective data, such as facts and figures, thereby eliminating bias.

exclamation point: a punctuation mark used to indicate surprise or excitement; can be used correctly after a word, phrase, or complete sentence. (Use exclamation points sparingly (or not at all) for academic and professional writing.)

external due date: a project completion date specified by the person or agency commissioning the project. Compare **internal due date**.

F

feedback: an objective appraisal based on specific details that offers a constructive description rather than a vague summary. Compare **evaluation**. See also **constructive feedback** and **objective feedback**.

filler: an empty word that adds no value to a message (e.g., "just" and "like").

flowchart: a graphic representation of information that depicts progression through a procedure or system.

font: the style of typeface, such as Times or Arial. Fonts number in the hundreds, and each word processing program includes its own series of fonts. See also **serif** and **sans serif**.

format: the overall appearance of a document, including placement of the entire text and individual parts (e.g., dateline and salutation) and the use of special features and white space.

fragment: a phrase or dependent clause that is incorrectly punctuated as a complete sentence.

freewriting: a writing technique that involves writing thoughts freely in a stream of consciousness to release feelings and stress and gain insight.

fused sentence: a grammatical error in which two independent clauses are connected without a comma or conjunction.

G

gender bias: in writing, the exclusion of one gender by using only masculine or feminine pronouns in contexts that apply to both genders. APA style accepts the plural pronoun "they" as a singular third-person pronoun.

gender: a social construct that refers to the attitudes, feelings, and behaviors a given culture associates with a person's biological sex; use the term "gender" when referring to people as social groups.

genderism: the belief that there are only two genders and that gender is automatically linked to an individual's sex assigned at birth.

gender identity: a person's psychological sense of their own gender.

gender-fluid: a person who is nonbinary and whose gender varies from presumptions based on their sex assigned at birth.

gerund: the "-ing" form of a verb (e.g., "seeing," "going," or "following"); functions as a noun.

gerund phrase: a gerund followed by a preposition, noun, and any modifiers (e.g., "going to the meeting" and "being on time"); functions as a noun.

global communication: communication across language and cultural borders.

grammatical subject: a subject that generally precedes the verb but may or may not be the actor or agent that performs the action of the verb; in an active-voice sentence, the same as the real subject. Compare **real subject**.

groupthink: a phenomenon in which everyone "goes along to get along," agreeing with decisions regardless of quality; occurs when a need for approval (or a fear of disapproval) exists among members.

growing edge: An area in which a person needs more expertise or experience. Also called "weakness."

H

hard copy: a paper copy of a document (as compared to an electronic copy). Compare **soft copy**.

hedge: a word or phrase that qualifies a statement by making it less than universal (e.g., "sort of" and "kind of"); can weaken the message, so should be used sparingly.

helper verb: See **auxiliary**.

highly formal (writing): a style of writing characterized by use of the passive voice, complicated language, abstract references, no contractions, and Latin abbreviations.

Hispanic: a broad term that refers to persons of Spanish-speaking origin or ancestry who share a connection to Spain.

hypothesis: an explanation that can be tested.

I

idiom: an expression peculiar to a language, not readily analyzable from its grammatical construction or from the meaning of its component parts; for example, "to put up with" translates to "tolerate or endure." See **colloquial**.

identity-first language: language that focuses on a disability or chronic condition, such as "substance abusers" or "the disabled." In general, person-first language is preferred.

independent clause: a clause that has a subject and verb and expresses a complete thought; can stand alone as a sentence.

indirect approach: in written communications, a style that presents details and explanations before getting to the main point; often used in messages that convey bad or unwelcome news. Compare **direct approach**.

indirect practice: a practice that involves indirect contact with clients, such as social work administration that is conducted on behalf of clients but does not usually involve direct contact with them.

infinitive: the base form of the verb preceded by "to" (for example, "to be," "to see," and "to speak"); functions as a noun, adjective, or adverb.

infinitive phrase: an infinitive along with an object and any modifiers (e.g., "to go to the store" or "to see the latest book reviews"); functions as a noun, adjective, or adverb.

informal speech: the language pattern used for speaking in everyday situations, as compared to doing a formal presentation; does not adhere strictly to standard rules of English usage.

information flow: in writing, the transition between ideas. Presenting old information that leads to new information creates smooth transitions and ensures that messages are cohesive and coherent.

initialism: an abbreviation pronounced letter by letter (e.g., IBM and NYPD).

internal due date: a project completion date that group members set among themselves to ensure they will meet external requirements. Compare **external due date**.

intransitive verb: a verb that cannot transfer action to a direct object. Compare **transitive verb**.

introductory paragraph: in a letter, the opening paragraph; connects the reader with the writer's purpose.

irregular verb: a verb that forms its past and past participle in an irregular way (e.g., fly, flew, flown; sink, sank, sunk).

J

jargon: using initials, abbreviations, technical, or occupational terminology as a sort of verbal shorthand.

job search profile: a compilation of information about a person's skills, qualities, interests, education, and employment history; serves as the basis for a résumé, job search, and job interviews.

K

keyword summary: a list of words and terms that reflect the content of an abstract, article, or other type of document or a list of skills on a résumé; used to identify a document in search results.

L

Latino/Latina: persons of Latin American heritage or origin who share a history of colonization from Spain.

linking verb: See **state-of-being verb**.

listener: in the communication process, the receiver of a message.

M

macro: a large social system such as a formal organization or community.

main verb: the last verb in a string of verbs. In English, as many as five verbs can string together to form meaning.

meta discourse: as coined by Joseph Williams, author of *Style*, a term that refers to the language a writer uses to describe their own thinking process; usually consists of unnecessary information.

method: the "how," "when," "where," and "who" of accomplishing a project.

Mexican: citizen of Mexico.

micro: a small social system, such as a social group or family.

mirroring: paraphrasing what the speaker said to ensure the message was received clearly.

modifier: a word or group of words that describes another word.

N

narrative citation: an in-text citation in which the author's name is integrated into a sentence as part of the narrative. Compare **parenthetical citation**.

networking: engaging in social and professional activities that facilitate interaction with people who can provide assistance with one's career or problem-solving endeavors.

new information: unfamiliar information; information that extends the reader's understanding.

nominal: a noun that originated as a verb; often formed by adding "-tion" or "ment" to the base form of the verb (e.g., "development" from the verb "develop").

nominative case: also called "subjective case." The form of pronouns that function as subjects of verbs. Subject pronouns must be followed by a verb (either real or implied).

nonbinary gender: a term that refers to a person who is gender-fluid, genderqueer, gender-nonconforming, gender-neutral, agender, and so on.

null hypothesis: a hypothesis that is negated, so statistical analysis can be used to disprove it, showing the likelihood that the original hypothesis is valid.

O

object: a word, phrase, or clause that follows a verb and receives the action of the verb.

objective case: the form of pronouns that function as objects of verbs or prepositions (e.g., me, him, her, or them).

old information: familiar information; information that is obvious or that the reader already knows; creates a context for new information.

open punctuation: in letters, a style of punctuation in which no punctuation follows the salutation and the complimentary closing.

P

paraphrase: putting someone else's ideas or words into one's own words; requires a citation to the original source. Incorrect paraphrasing (making a few changes in word order, leaving out a word or two, or substituting similar words) is a form of plagiarism.

parenthetical citation: an in-text citation in which the author and date are in parentheses, usually at the end of the sentence. (Compare **narrative citation.**)

passive voice: as applied to verbs, a term indicating that the subject does not perform the action of the verb (e.g., "The report *was written* by Bob"— the subject, "report," did not perform the action, "was written"). Compare **active voice**.

past: the simple past form of a verb, used without a helper verb (e.g., "worked," "did," "was," and "followed").

past participle: a verb form that consists of the past form preceded by a helper verb (e.g., "have worked," "had done," "have been," and "had followed").

PEER model: a guide to structuring information while composing or revising: define purpose, provide evidence, give an explanation or examples, and recap main points.

period: a punctuation mark used to indicate the end of a statement; also used with some abbreviations and with Web addresses. Also called a "dot."

person-first language: language that emphasizes the person, not the person's disability or chronic condition; for example, "people with substance use disorders" or "people with disabilities." In general, person-first language is preferred over identity-first language.

phrase: a group of words that form a unit but do not usually include a subject and a verb and cannot stand alone as a sentence; functions as a noun, adjective, or adverb. Types include prepositional, gerund, and infinitive phrases, among others.

pie charts: a graphics tool that displays information as "slices" of a circle; enables the reader to easily see both the relationship of one item to another and the relationships of all parts to the whole.

plagiarism: the use of another's ideas or words without crediting the source; constitutes a form of stealing. (The term is derived from the Latin *plagiarius*, meaning "an abductor" or "thief.")

portfolio: for a job search, a collection of pertinent documents and information (e.g., purpose statements, résumés, work samples, reference letters, networking contacts, and business cards).

possessive case: the form of pronouns that show possession of nouns or other pronouns (e.g., "my," "mine," "his," "her," "hers," "its," and "their").

prioritizing: identifying the rank order of items in a list; identifying the level of importance.

process message: a message used to communicate progress on an assignment; a communication tool to use as a learning resource. Format a process message as an e-mail, using a subject line, greeting, and closing.

professional writing: a direct style of writing characterized by use of the active voice; simple words; personal pronouns (e.g., "I," "you," and "we"); and, at times, contractions (e.g., "can't" for "cannot"); used in most business communications. Compare **highly formal**.

progressive tenses: verb tenses in which the main verb ends in "-ing" and is preceded by a helper verb; used to indicate continuous action in the past, present, or future.

pronoun: a word (e.g., "I," "you," "he," "she," "it," "we," and "they") used in place of a noun or another pronoun; must agree with its antecedent in number, person, and gender.

pronoun viewpoint: the point of view that emanates from the number, person, and gender of a subjective case pronoun (e.g., the "I" or "you" viewpoint); should be consistent within sentences; paragraphs; and, at times, documents.

proofread: correcting the grammar, punctuation, spelling, and word usage; part of the editing process but also stands on its own as the final, critical step in producing a document.

proofreader's marks: a table of established marks that editors and printers use to show changes in a document.

protocols: formalities and rules of order and etiquette; play an important role in global business, governing interactions such as introductions, greetings, and written communications.

purpose statement: a few sentences discussing why a topic was selected and why it is important, answering the question "So what?" A purpose statement introduces a thesis statement.

Q

qualitative research: research that involves collecting narrative data to gain insight into phenomena of interest; often done by administering surveys and questionnaires.

quantify: expressing numerically; a way to describe an achievement or goal (e.g., as a percentage, length of time, or amount of money) that shows its contribution to the bottom line.

quantitative research: research that involves collecting numerical data to explain, predict, and/or control phenomena of interest; often done by applying the scientific method, with experimental and control groups.

question mark: a punctuation mark used to indicate a question the writer expects the reader to answer; sometimes can occur after individual words as well as complete sentences structured as questions.

R

random sampling: a research technique in which the researcher surveys a group of people who are chosen at random and thus believed to be representative of the broader population; reduces bias and enables calculation of a margin of error.

real subject: the actor or agent that performs the action of the verb but may or may not appear in the sentence; in an active sentence, the same as the grammatical subject. Compare **grammatical subject**.

reflexive case: the form of pronouns that reflect back to subjective case pronouns (e.g., "myself," "yourself," and "ourselves"). Also called **intensive case**.

regular verb: a verb that forms its past and past participle by adding "–ed" to the base (e.g., "walk," "walked," and "have walked").

reliability: in research, consistency of measure; for example, if the same study is repeated several times and the outcomes are the same, then it is reliable.

research: the process of investigating, inquiring, and examining; involves seeking answers in a methodical, objective manner that includes an established line of thought and credible experience.

resistance: a barrier consisting of beliefs, attitudes, and behaviors that keeps people from moving forward with a decision; can stem from tangible sources (e.g., lack of resources) or intangible sources (e.g., lack of trust) and from valid or invalid concerns.

revise: improving the way written ideas are presented by moving sentences or paragraphs and ensuring major parts of the document achieve what is intended; intertwined with editing as the document progresses but on its own as a final check before proofreading.

run-on sentence: a sentence that consists of two independent clauses joined with insufficient punctuation, such as with only one comma.

S

"-s" form: the third-person singular form of a verb in simple present tense (e.g., "works," "does," and "follows").

salutation: the opening greeting of a letter or e-mail message.

sans-serif: a font in which (e.g., Arial or Calibri) the top and bottom of the letters are uniform in thickness and look flat; literally, "without the line." Compare **serif**.

scientific method: a rigorous process used to identify predictability of hypotheses in quantitative research, including a control group and an experimental group.

scholastic writing: See **academic writing**.

semicolon: a punctuation mark used to separate two independent clauses and sometimes items in a series; stronger than a comma but weaker than a period; can be considered a "full stop that is not terminal."

sentence: a group of words that has a subject and a verb and expresses a complete thought; an independent clause.

sentence case: capitalizing the first word of the title and the first word following a colon (e.g., a subtitle) as well as proper nouns and adjectives; all other words are typed in lowercase. Compare **title case**.

serif: a font in which the edges of the letters end in short lines, creating a pointed or sharp look (e.g., Times New Roman). Compare **sans-serif**.

set of commas: a pair of commas that set off nonessential information in a sentence.

singular "they": the use of the pronoun "they" and its derivative forms ("them," "their," "theirs," "themselves," and "theirselves") as gender-neutral singular pronouns. For academic writing, the singular "they" (but not its derivative forms) is typically used with an unspecified antecedent, such as "teacher" or "researcher."

soft copy: an electronic version of a document. Compare **hard copy**.

Spanish: a language; also refers to people born in Spain.

speaker: in the communication process, the sender of a message.

standard punctuation: in letters, a punctuation style in which a colon follows the salutation and a comma follows the complimentary closing; the most common for business letters.

state-of-being verb: a verb that does not transfer action but instead links a subject to a subject complement (rather than direct object); any form of "to be" ("is," "are," "was," and "were"), "appear," "become," and "seem" and, at times, "smell," "taste," "feel," "sound," "look," "act," and "grow." Also called a **linking verb**.

strategy: an approach to solving problems or accomplishing a vision that consists of developing goals, objectives, and action plans.

style: in writing, the overall manner of presentation in a document; determined by many individual writing decisions that contribute to the total effect.

subheading: a minor heading; a heading for a subsection.

subject: together with the verb, the core of a sentence; can be a noun, phrase, or clause. See also **grammatical subject** and **real subject**.

subjective case: the form of pronouns that function as subjects of verbs. Subject pronouns must be followed by a verb (either real or implied). Also called **nominative case**.

subordinating conjunctions: a word or phrase (e.g., "if," "when," "as," "although," "because," "as soon as," and "before") used to connect a dependent clause to an independent clause; defines the relationship between the ideas in the clauses.

subjunctive mood: the form of the verb used to express a condition that is improbable, highly unlikely, or contrary to fact; also used with certain requests, demands, recommendations, and set phrases.

subsystem: a component element of a focal system that displays all the attributes of a system but can be located within a larger designate system; for example, a married couple functions as a system and is a subsystem of the total family unit.

summary: on a résumé, the section that highlights one's experience, achievements, and greatest skills and abilities.

superlative form: the form of an adjective used when three or more items are compared; for regular adjectives, formed by adding the suffix "-est" or using "most" or "least" before the adjective.

survey: a research tool in which a questionnaire is administered to a number of people; designed to elicit responses about a specific topic being studied.

synergy: the energy created in team dynamics that leads to the whole becoming more than the sum of its parts.

synopsis: a short, written statement that gives an overview of a report, study, or proposal; used in academic writing but equivalent to an abstract or executive summary.

syntax: the orderly arrangements of words. Also called **grammar**.

T

table: a graphics tool that displays data in columns and rows.

tag-on: an unnecessary preposition at the end of a phrase or clause; for example, "Where do you live *at*?"

thesis statement: a one- or two-sentence summary of the problem being discussed or argument being made in a paper.

title case: setting titles in uppercase and lowercase letters, with the following guidelines for capitalization: capitalize all words in the title except for articles, conjunctions, and prepositions of three or fewer letters. Compare **sentence case**.

topic sentence: a broad, general sentence that gives an overview of the paragraph.

topic string: a series of sentences that develop the specific idea presented in a topic sentence.

transferable skills: qualities, skills, and expertise that characterize a person regardless of job description or profession and, thus, transfer with the person from one job to another.

transgender: a term used to refer to persons whose gender identity does not conform to what is culturally associated with their sex assigned at birth.

transnegativity or transprejudice: terms that denote discriminatory attitudes toward individuals who are transgender.

TGNC: an abbreviation for "transgender, nonconforming"

transitional paragraph: in a document, a paragraph that summarizes the key ideas of the current section and indicates how the major theme of the document will be developed in the next section.

transitional sentence: a sentence that provides a logical connection between paragraphs.

V

validity: in research, whether a study examines what it is intended to examine.

value: a belief pertaining to what is right and good, comprising the normative structure of a social system; for example, values form the foundation on which social systems develop.

verb: together with the subject, the core or nucleus of a sentence; conjugated on the basis of subject and tense. Verb usage indicates whether an event happened in the past, is happening in the present, or will happen in the future. See also **action verb**, **intransitive verb**, **state-of-being verb**, and **transitive verb**.

visual persuasion: incorporating special features such as bold, underlining, italics, numbering, and bullet points, so key points are instantly visible to the reader.

voicemail: recorded phone messages.

W

"we" viewpoint: in written messages, a pronoun point of view that expresses teamwork and indicates that the ideas are those of the company as well as the writer; frequently used in business today.

works-cited list: in the MLA reference style, the end-of-document references list; equivalent to a bibliography.

Y

"you" viewpoint: in written messages, a pronoun point of view that helps the writer connect with the reader and focus on the reader's needs.

INDEX

Printed in the USA
CPSIA information can be obtained
at www.ICGtesting.com
LVHW012058290324
775781LV00010B/4

9 781793 581556